MW00618267

Warm Springs Millennium

Warm Springs Millennium

VOICES FROM THE RESERVATION

MICHAEL BAUGHMAN AND CHARLOTTE HADELLA

University of Texas Press

AUSTIN

Copyright © 2000 by the University of Texas Press

All rights reserved
Printed in the United States of America

First edition, 2000

Requests for permission to reproduce material from this work
should be sent to Permissions, University of Texas Press, Box
7819, Austin, TX 78713-7819.

⊗ The paper used in this book meets the minimum requirements
of ANSI/NISO Z39.48-1992 (R1997) (Permanence of Paper).

LIBRARY OF CONGRESS CATALOGING-IN-PUBLICATION DATA
Baughman, Mike.
Warm Springs millennium: voices from the reservation /
Michael Baughman and Charlotte Hadella. — 1st ed.
        p.   cm.
Includes bibliographical references and index.
ISBN 0-292-70885-8 (cloth : alk. paper) — ISBN 0-292-70886-6
(pbk. : alk. paper)
      1. Indians of North America — Oregon — Warm Springs
Indian Reservation.   2. Warm Springs Indian Reservation (Or.)
I. Hadella, Charlotte Cook.   II. Title.
E78.O6 B38   2000
979.5′62 — dc21   00-021339

For Lucia, Billy, Dana, and Jake, the next generation

Contents

Introduction   1

The Eagle's Thorn   12

The Seasonal Round   21

Brent Florendo   35

One Thousand Square Miles   44

James Hall   58

Sue Terran   64

Wilson Wewa Jr.   74

Stoney Miller   92

Lillian Brunoe   107

Dawn Smith   118

Helena Jackson   125

The Deserted Boy   133

Foster Kalama   148

Afterword   161

Suggested Reading   165

Index   169

Warm Springs Millennium

Introduction

One hopes; one hopes against hope that somehow it will make a little difference; only a little, but still some, if people mostly unknown to almost all of us get better known to more of us.

ROBERT COLES, *Eskimos, Chicanos, Indians*

About twenty years ago, these were the very first words I ever heard from a Warm Springs Indian:

"You want some ice to cool your balls off?"

This was a warm evening in June, and I was somewhere not far from Trout Creek, tying leader sections together with blood knots and waiting to be picked up by a guide in a drift boat. The guide and I would be fishing the Deschutes River for two days, and I was on assignment from *Sports Illustrated* to do an article on the experience.

(In late spring stone flies hatch on the Deschutes, clumsily flying two-inch-long insects that fall by the thousands into the river, often sending even big trout into uncharacteristically reckless feeding binges.)

The three young Indian men (they were in their early twenties; I was in my early forties) had arrived silently and taken seats on a large flat-topped rock no more than twenty feet from my rock, and I had no idea how long they had been there, watching me struggle with my blood knots. On the dusty ground in front of them was a small Styrofoam cooler, and two of the young men reached in and pulled out cans of root beer just as I looked up. I also noticed three old fiberglass fly rods with beat-up Pflueger reels lying behind the cooler.

"I don't need any ice," I finally said.

"You sure?" asked the one without a root beer — the same one who had asked the original question.

"I'm sure," I said.

"You going to fish around here?"

"As soon as the guy I'm meeting shows up."

"You got to buy a permit to fish the river along the reservation."

"I already bought it," I said, "at the Rainbow Market." I smiled at him then—at the three of them—and somehow, luckily, the bad moment passed.

By the time the sound of an aluminum boat hull sliding over gravel announced the arrival of the guide, they had given me one of their six cans of root beer. In trade, I had given them a half-dozen orange-bodied stone fly imitations from the boxful I'd tied for the trip the week before.

Within seconds after I'd climbed into the boat and we were out into the heavy pull of the river current, the guide, another young man, looked at me quizzically.

"Where'd those three come from?" he asked.

"I don't know. I didn't ask them."

"Well, you don't want to fool with these local boys around here any more than you have to. Sometimes they act like they own the damn river."

"Don't they?" I asked.

"Well, maybe the half on their side—but that's all."

The Deschutes fishing was productive, with stone flies plentiful and rainbow trout, locally called "redsides," rising aggressively nearly everywhere from morning to night; but the river was too crowded with rafters and other anglers for me to enjoy it. I didn't really like the guide much either, and though I never heard from him about it, I'm certain he didn't care for the article I wrote. But I never got the young men with the root beer out of my mind, and I knew for certain I'd be back to Warm Springs and the Deschutes.

Eventually I wrote a book titled *Mohawk Blood*, which, among other things, is a narrative account of the influence that my great-grandfather John Brant, a descendant of Mohawk chief Joseph Brant, has had on my life. The book ends with a chapter about my grandson Billy, the point being that this relationship is one way a heritage survives. Through what I say to Billy, what I teach him, and, most important, what I do with him, the things I learned from John Brant are passed ahead to yet another generation.

TOP *The Deschutes River near Dry Creek*
ABOVE *The Rainbow Market* (AUTHOR PHOTOS)

Now as we near the end of another century, this seems to me to be an awfully important subject as it relates generally to North American Indians, and to all other thoughtful Americans as well. After the broken treaties and massacres of the nineteenth century and the continued betrayal and then neglect of the twentieth, who *are* American Indians now, and what will likely become of them and their traditional ways of life in the years ahead?

The Warm Springs Reservation in north-central Oregon is probably as good a place as any in America to seek out likely answers to these questions. An area of just about one thousand square miles, the reservation is home to about thirty-six hundred Indians, principally the Warm Springs, Wascos, and Paiutes, with approximately half of this population under twenty years of age.

The Deschutes River, which constitutes the eastern border of the reservation, is one of the Columbia River's major tributaries and is such a big, powerful river in its own right that it seems distinctly out of place in this dry country of volcanic rock and talus slopes, sage brush and juniper. In some fairly obvious ways, the Deschutes stands as a telling benchmark of how the Pacific Northwest has changed over the past century.

For thousands of years, the Indians of the Northwest fished the Pacific and its coastal streams. They ate fresh fish during the seasonal runs, dried and smoked it for winter use, and pounded it into a powdery meal that, mixed with dried berries and fruits, became a staple food called pemmican. Their fishing methods included nets made of willow bark, traps and weirs, dip nets and spears, and the bow and arrow. The runs of fish in different rivers and creeks might have fluctuated from year to year, but the overall abundance never varied.

Then white men arrived in numbers during the nineteenth century, and by 1920 the salmon harvests in the Northwest averaged about 240 million pounds per year. For the past decade, harvests have averaged about 10 million pounds, and the fish runs continue to decline. At least half of the native trout, steelhead, and salmon populations of the Northwest are already extinct. There are seventy-nine dams on the Columbia River system, and each year they kill more than 90 percent of the juvenile steelhead and salmon attempting to migrate downstream to the Pacific. (A radio commercial played on many Oregon stations in 1996 promised without a hint of irony that "on our Columbia River cruise, you rise and rise through eight majestic dams.")

Oregon Trout, a conservation organization widely known for its accuracy, estimates that over 90 percent of all the water in the Deschutes River basin is consumed by irrigation and livestock. So, like many other waterways, the Deschutes is a dying river. Unless Americans change their ways in a hurry, the salmon will go the way of the passenger pigeon and buffalo; for the native peoples whose very lives have always been centered around the coastal rivers and their fish, this is certainly tragic. Can cultures hope to survive once their very roots have been destroyed?

Two centuries ago Indians of the Northwest were, without much doubt, as free as any people on earth. But the last "wild" Indian in America, a Yahi who became known as Ishi, walked out of northern California's Mill Creek canyon in 1911. What, then, *is* an Indian today?

Not long ago I was told by a Lakota Sioux named Robert Owens that "heart and language are what matter." N. Scott Momaday has written that "an Indian is an idea which a given man has of himself. And it is a moral idea, for it accounts for the way which he reacts to other men and to the world in general. And that idea, in order to be realized completely, has to be expressed."

I used a simple, straightforward quotation from a Quinalt leader named Joe Delacruz in *Mohawk Blood:* "People get into language and dance and songs and stuff, powwows, and they think that's culture. How much of the Quinalt culture is left? I see about two hundred and fifty people—they're fishing, they're happy, they're doing what our ancestors did. They get their deer; they get their elk. They live the way they want to live. That's more culture than the powwow dancing thing." (I used the quotation because I tend to believe it: By far the sharpest and most necessary edge of the subsistence hunter's arrowhead was knowledge, and no one will ever again know this continent as he did.)

So, yes, it is a complex subject that can be approached from many directions, and confusions and controversies are definitely inevitable.

More than twenty years ago, a friend of mine named Doug Latimer, then a vice president at Harper and Row, edited a series of Native American books by such authors as James Welch and Duane Niatum. The first title published in the series was *Seven Arrows*, by Hyemeyohsts Storm, a Northern Cheyenne born at the Lame Deer Agency in Montana. Latimer was convinced the book was a good and important one, but Rupert Castro, president of the American Indian Historical Society, attacked it vigorously in a review published in *The Indian Historian* (Summer 1972, Vol. 5, No. 2).

"This book, *Seven Arrows*, will bring disgrace to Harper and Row," Castro wrote. He even expressed doubt that Storm, though enrolled as a Northern Cheyenne, was indeed a "real Indian." ". . .[A]n enrollment number doth not an Indian make!" Castro argued. "Quite a few Anglos and Blacks were adopted into Indian tribes. Sometimes, as in the case of the Blacks, the Indians were forced by the U.S. Government to accept them on the tribal rolls. In other cases such as the Osage, whites were fraudulently enrolled, with the active help of the Bureau of Indian Affairs."

Toward the end of the review, Latimer receives his only mention: "It is most unfortunate that the author, who has no religious or secular status in the tribe, is so presumptuous as to bestow Indian names upon his white benefactors, among whom is Mr. Douglas Latimer, his mentor and a vice president of Harper and Row."

The last line of the review accuses Storm of "vulgarizing one of the most beautiful but least known religions of man."

It is worth relating all of this because I happen to know beyond any doubt that Doug Latimer cared very deeply about North American Indians and their problems and causes. He ran Harper and Row's Native American Publishing Program on his own time, with all profits donated to Native American causes.

(A few years before he began the publishing program, Latimer had purchased two thousand acres of land in the Mill Creek canyon east of Red Bluff, California, the very same Yahi land from which Ishi had emerged. Latimer's primary reason for buying the land—and going into what he called "lifelong debt"—was to protect it from developers and thereby save the traces that remain of Yahi culture.)

Largely as a result of Castro's review, Latimer actually learned the Cheyenne language and traveled to Wyoming to discuss *Seven Arrows*—to try to justify the book—with a tribal dignitary. While Latimer and the elder spoke in Cheyenne, the Indian's two young sons sat in the next room watching *Star Trek* on television.

This entire episode, from Hyemeyohsts Storm through Rupert

Castro and Doug Latimer to *Star Trek*, asks many more questions than it answers, and they are important questions.

White attitudes toward Indians range from liberalism (sometimes of the comically blind New Age variety, sometimes responsible and even useful) to the worst sort of racism. I once heard these extremes demonstrated in a few minutes of conversation at a café in Custer, South Dakota, not far from the Pine Ridge Reservation. One customer, a middle-aged man I took for a farmer, expressed the opinion that when whites took over the continent, it was nothing less than a case of the most materialistic people in the history of the earth supplanting a population spiritually, morally, and physically superior to their own. Only superior numbers and technology could ever have defeated such warriors as Crazy Horse. This struck me as quite a speech, and it was promptly answered by a younger man, skinny and long-haired, with tattoos on his arms, whose reply was that Pine Ridge Indians were "prairie niggers," and as far as he was concerned, that was that.

Even given our continent's history, the attitudes of the most enlightened Indians toward whites can be surprisingly vicious. A friend of mine published a not unfavorable review of a novel written by a resident of Pine Ridge, to which the novel's author responded in a letter calling my friend a "Mutant Ninja literary fairy" and a "half-baked academic eunuch." And that was that.

Even the feuds and arguments among Indians themselves can be very complicated. At Pine Ridge I overheard two middle-aged men discussing the American Indian Movement (AIM) of the 1970s, which resulted both in Leonard Peltier's arrest and very controversial conviction for the murder of two FBI agents, and in the bombing by Indians of the court house in Custer.

One of the Pine Ridge men pointed out that the military action at Wounded Knee in 1975 was the largest use of troops on American soil since the Civil War, and he argued that the young and militant Indians involved (perhaps he was one of them) had given their people more pride in themselves than they had had at any other time in this century. But his companion argued that all AIM had really done was cause whites to hate Indians more than ever, and what good could possibly come of that? It was the whites' country now, wasn't it?

That question stopped the conversation cold.

I still fish the Deschutes occasionally despite the crowds, and I spend as much time as I can on the Warm Springs Reservation these days. I've hiked the rugged country and chased the mule deer and coveys of chukar up and down the steep slopes. I've listened to coyotes yap and howl at midnight along the Warm Springs River, answered by their brothers and sisters on the nearby sage and juniper hills. I've talked to the Warm Springs people, and I've even stayed at the Kah-Nee-Ta Lodge and lost a little money at the Indian Head Casino. I listen to "the station on the reservation," KWSO, which plays everything from drumming and chants to Madonna, and I keep up with the bimonthly reservation paper, *Spilyay Tymoo* (Coyote News). And I'm familiar with the nearby white communities too—Redmond, Madras, Maupin, and Willowdale—where I've drunk my share of bad draft beer, shot games of eight-ball, and joined, for better or worse, in the general conversation. My interest in the area and its people, both Indians and whites, came long before any serious idea for this book. The book, I suppose, is the result of having had John Brant as a great-grandfather, of growing up in Hawaii with very close friends from many cultures, and of that minor verbal run-in with the young man on the banks of the Deschutes.

Of at least equal importance is the fact that I met my co-author, Charlotte Hadella, a few years ago. An accomplished writer and scholar, she currently teaches Native American literature classes at Southern Oregon University in Ashland. She did nearly all of the considerable research that went into the project and also conducted many of our interviews.

The interviews were included for a simple reason. Anyone reading the transcribed speeches of American Indian leaders will likely be struck immediately by a use of words that is clear and honest, simple yet profound—often, in fact, poetic.

Consider this excerpt, from a nineteenth-century northwestern tribal chief: "The earth was created by the assistance of the sun, and it should be left as it was. . . . The country was made without

Kah-Nee-Ta Lodge (AUTHOR PHOTO)

lines of demarcation, and it is no man's business to divide it. . . . The earth and myself are of one mind. The measure of the land and the measure of our bodies are the same. Say to us if you can say it, that you were sent by the Creative Power to talk to us. Perhaps you think the Creator sent you here to dispose of us as you see fit. Do not misunderstand me, but understand me fully with reference to my affection for the land. I never said that land was mine to do with as I chose. The one who has the right to dispose of it is the one who created it. I claim a right to live on my land, and accord you the privilege to live on yours."

And then this (fairly typical, mercifully brief) statement from a twentieth-century candidate for the United States presidency, in his acceptance speech at the nominating convention: ". . . [A]ll things flow from doing what is right . . . only right conduct distinguish [*sic*] a great nation from that [*sic*] cannot rise above itself. I assure you, I guarantee it, when I say what I mean, I mean it. It has never been otherwise. . . ."

Perhaps this difference in public utterance is attributable to the Indians' long oral tradition. The spoken word mattered because it was what they had. In contrast, we now live in a country where not only do prominent politicians not write their own speeches, but they often have great difficulty even standing in front of a camera and coherently reading the clichés, lies, evasions, and abstractions composed for them by somebody else. In any event, today's American Indians often speak with much of the clarity and honesty their ancestors demonstrated. Our interviews concentrate on Warm Springs residents of early middle age, who are raising school-age children and are also in the process of assuming positions of crucial authority on the reservation; of course, we've talked to local whites too, because they are an inevitable component of modern Warm Springs life.

In one of our interviews, Brent Florendo, a Wasco, says, "What's out there now always seems to reflect back into our cultural past, for the most part. The only way the masses seem to be able to identify with us is in the past. My idea is: We're still here; we're a viable people; we have the same heartbreaks, the same successes, the same failures as everybody else does. . . . We're here yet, but it's like we're invisible, and it seems like it's always kind of been that way."

Brent makes this crucial point absolutely correctly. In my youth, Indians of the past were portrayed in the Saturday movies as (to borrow the title of one of Paiute Adrian Louis's volumes of poetry) "blood thirsty savages." The more recent and currently fashionable myth, exploited in *Dances with Wolves*, allows white Americans to feel a safe, sentimental nostalgia for Indians of long ago who, long and safely dead, have finally become noble. This new myth is at least as destructive as the old one, because it allows most Americans to avoid thinking about the Indians living today and to ignore what has been done to them. Obviously, reservations are in some ways nothing but rural ghettos. This is exactly why, as author Peter Matthiessen correctly points out in *In the Spirit of Crazy Horse*, ". . . most studies of Indian history and culture avoid mention of the twentieth century."

As admitted amateurs and outsiders, our intention here is to counter this trend, to offer an honest look at a twentieth-century reservation. In doing so, perhaps we will help prove that many of our real Indians, still living and suffering, always struggling, often succeeding, are worthy of recognition and respect.

We have included what we think is enough (and no more than enough) historical material concerning the formation of the reservation. After that we have outlined the traditional ways of life, the "seasonal rounds," which were lost as a result of the reservation. Brent Florendo's interview was included among these introductory chapters because he speaks, in a compelling personal voice, of the themes and subjects central to the entire book: the destruction of the Columbia River system, racism, the dilemma of living in two distinctly different worlds, and education. Our chapter on education, "The Deserted Boy," is placed among the interviews toward the end of the book, where education has become the central focus.

It became clear soon after we began to visit Warm Springs regularly that education as it pertains to native languages and the passing on of cultural traditions is at the heart of efforts to revitalize reservation life. We certainly don't pretend to have arrived at any unarguable conclusions about these issues. The diversity of our interviews, and their contradictions, are a reflection of the cultural complexities evident at Warm Springs. The imposition of an organization or contrived scheme that might imply that such a rich life can be compartmentalized and easily defined would have been both self-defeating and dishonest.

What we have done, as well as we could, is observe day-to-day life on the reservation and in nearby towns; and, most significantly, we have heard the Warm Springs people speak for themselves. They represent a group that has rarely had a public audience and that surely deserves one.

M. B.

The Eagle's Thorn

In the old time, the world was all dark. There was no sun out to give light; Eagle had it in a box, and he wouldn't let any of the other people come near it. He carried it in his claws.

So begins "The Sun Box," one of the ancient sunlight myths of the Warm Springs Indians collected by Jarold Ramsey in *Coyote Was Going There: Indian Literature of the Oregon Country.* The story explains, at least on one level, the daily cycle of light and dark. It identifies Eagle as a powerful entity, designated by the Creator to be the keeper of the light.

The tale goes on to explain that in this primordial time, other mythic animal people besides Eagle know about sunlight and long for it because, occasionally, Eagle opens the lid of the sun box and illuminates the earth for just a moment. Tired of living in darkness, the earth people repeatedly ask Eagle to let the sun out of the box. For reasons not stated explicitly in the story, Eagle ignores these pleas.

Finally, however, Eagle is forced to call on his fellow creatures for help when he alights on a thorn tree and severely injures his foot. Crow, the healer, agrees to treat Eagle's wound if he can have light by which to work. So Eagle, though suspicious, allows Crow to open the sun box just a little.

Right then Crow grabbed the box in his claws, flew up high with it, and, cawing in triumph, dropped it to smash against the rocks far below. The sunlight went free and filled the world.

Like many of the traditional stories passed down orally through generations of tribal peoples, "The Sun Box" communicates important messages about the ethics, values, and world view of the culture that produced it. More specifically, the story can serve as a useful touchstone in an examination of the Confederated Tribes of the Warm Springs Reservation: the reservation's history, its current status in terms of the issues raised in the introduction, and its hopes for the future.

Besides explaining how daylight came to be, "The Sun Box" also raises questions: Why does Eagle show the people the light if he really intends to withhold it from them forever? Is he simply preparing the people for what is to come? Must they experience prolonged darkness so that ultimately they will truly appreciate sunlight? Must they be exposed gradually to light, or whatever it may symbolize (knowledge, spirituality, tradition), to avoid the shock of immediate, total exposure to something overwhelming? If the world hadn't been dark, would Eagle have landed on the thorn and hurt himself?

Indian storytelling was, and still is, not only entertainment, but also an important tool for moral and cultural instruction. "The Sun Box" comments on the distribution of power and resources, the destructive nature of selfishness, and the appropriate responses to the needs and suffering of others. The story also implies that change involves relinquishing power, that pain may accompany change, and that the agent of change may be neither wise nor benevolent. Finally, a natural balance is established as the result of the story's dramatic, somewhat ironical events. Surely children hearing "The Sun Box" again and again during the winter longhouse gatherings of pre-reservation time internalized these important lessons.

For thousands of years, the indigenous peoples of the Pacific Northwest enjoyed a relatively stable, unchanging lifestyle characterized by devotion to family, community, and religion; but by the mid-nineteenth century, the invasion of settlers brought irrevocable changes. The ability to accept these changes, and wherever possible to turn them to advantage, has been a valuable characteristic of the Warm Springs people.

Uprooted from their homes along the Columbia River, the Wascos and the Warm Springs Indians, in the Treaty of 1855, relinquished their claim to one-sixth of the land mass of Oregon and accepted a living area equaling one-fifteenth of their original territory. At this point much of the old life—hunting, fishing, gathering—became impractical if not impossible, and as a result, the preservation of oral literature became more important than ever to the tribal elders. (It has remained thus: In 1976, Elsie Pistolhead, an elderly Columbia River Indian, recorded in the Sahaptin language, from memory, sixteen hours of Coyote stories—nearly seventy myths set in primordial time.)

A central irony reverberates throughout this long, painful drama: reservations, though clearly designed as temporary concessions to Indians who resisted assimilation, and ultimately aimed at containing tribal power and civilizing "renegades," today have become the sanctuaries for the revitalization of North American Indian cultures. Reservations are the only true hope for passing tribal traditions on to future generations. Like Crow's deceptive theft of the sun box under the guise of lending aid, the United States government and its agents, in attempting to erase native cultures in order to save savages from primitivism, have established the means for preserving at least a portion of the traditional knowledge and practices they wanted to obliterate. When Crow was scheming to acquire the sun box, he certainly did not intend to set the sun free to shine on all of his fellow creatures; nevertheless, as a result of Crow's chicanery, the people received what they had long desired.

Though the Treaty of 1855 guaranteed the Warm Springs Indians access to traditional hunting, gathering, and fishing grounds, the aboriginal practice of living by the "seasonal round" had to be severely modified. For centuries, the Wascos and the Warm Springs peoples, both of whom have their origins in the Columbia Plateau culture, wintered near the Columbia River and then established spring camps a few miles away where bitterroot and other foods could be gathered. They camped at Celilo Falls (now inundated) for the spring and summer salmon runs and organized late summer berrying and hunting expeditions in the mountains. Archaeologists find evidence of these activities dating back at least ten thousand years.

Even though they spoke separate languages (the Warm Springs, Sahaptin; the Wascos, Chinookan), the two tribes are closely related socially and culturally. The Wascos, who were principally fishermen and traders, took a leading role in a major trade fair at

Celilo Falls every summer. They were a friendly and hospitable people, accustomed to dealing with different language groups, so it isn't difficult to understand how the Wascos and Warm Springs people have managed to wed their destinies and survive, even thrive, on the same reservation for nearly 150 years.

The third tribe of the confederation, the Northern Paiutes, joined the reservation in 1880. The Paiutes spoke a Shoshonean language, had traditionally ranged in the Great Basin region, and were enemies of the Plateau Indians. All three groups organized their existence according to seasonal rounds determined by available food supplies; but the foods and rounds differed according to the respective geographical areas.

Less inclined than other groups to accept the invasion and devastation of their homelands by white settlers, the Paiutes continued to raid neighboring Indian and white communities into the second half of the nineteenth century, in an effort to survive. During the 1860s, the United States launched military campaigns against the Paiutes that finally resulted in the negotiation of an 1868 peace treaty, which neither established a reservation for them nor provided them with any goods or services.

Finally, in 1872, President Grant set aside the Mallheur Indian Reservation in southeastern Oregon for the Paiutes; but by 1882, not one Paiute remained on the reservation, and President Garfield returned the land to public domain. Some of the Paiutes had joined the Bannocks from Idaho in fighting the U.S. Army, while others had been imprisoned at Fort Vancouver. When the federal government released the thirty-eight Paiute prisoners from Fort Vancouver in 1879, many of them moved to the Warm Springs Reservation, where they were later joined by more than seventy Paiutes from Yakima. The newcomers were extended all the rights and privileges of the Warm Springs and Wascos, even though they were not original treaty signers.

Describing the arrival in Warm Springs of the first Paiutes, Indian Agent John Smith wrote:

> *I received . . . a request from Gen. O. O. Howard . . . to come to his headquarters at Vancouver Barracks . . . regarding a small band of Paiute prisoners held by him. Anticipating what his object might be, [tribal]*

*members here voluntarily told me that if these Indians wanted to come
here, to bring them home with me. . . . My Indians will give them all
assistance possible, and [will have] the most friendly feeling toward
them which is remarkable since but a few years ago they were inveterate
enemies.*

The gesture of kindness and acceptance that led to the Paiutes'
inclusion in the Warm Springs Reservation harks back to lessons of
appropriate behavior gleaned from a story like "The Sun Box." By
withholding the sunlight from his brothers, Eagle lived in darkness
and suffered an injury because of it. Had he shared his gift initially,
he could have avoided both personal pain and humiliation.

When the Indian Reorganization Act of 1934 (also known as the
Wheeler-Howard Act) ended the policy of allotting reservation
lands, the Wascos, Warm Springs, and Paiute Indians formed a confederation and accepted a corporate charter from the United States
for their business endeavors. In 1937 they renamed themselves The
Confederated Tribes of the Warm Springs Reservation of Oregon
and created a constitution by which they still govern themselves
today. Under this constitution the Tribal Council is the central
governing body; it consists of eleven members, eight of whom are
elected to three-year terms, and three of whom are tribal chiefs —
one from each of the tribes — who serve life terms. Although the
council has legislative, executive, and judicial authority, it dele-
gates executive power to the General Manager and judicial power
to the Tribal Court. The Confederated Tribes operates its own forest products manufacturing plant, a hotel resort and casino, and
a clothing-textile industry. The Warm Springs Reservation also
boasts the first Indian-owned hydroelectric plant in the nation.

When European settlers began to inhabit North America, very
few of them seriously considered the impact their presence would
have on the people who already occupied the land. Though they
may have been impressed, even awed, by the beauty and richness of
the New World, they clearly believed that natural resources were
unlimited, that wilderness was something to overcome and Indians something to be rid of. Viewed either as obstacles to progress
or as heathens to be civilized, or both, tribal peoples had no hope
of influencing the shape or direction of the new nation. This cul-

ture clash, rooted deeply in irreconcilable differences of world view, community, family, and religion, was an obviously hopeless situation for Indians, pitted as they were against both the weaponry and diseases of a rapidly expanding European population.

Yet in spite of the fact that most settlers ignored the human rights of Indians, and even in some cases their very existence, some tribal groups refused to vanish into the wilderness, thus creating the need for a government policy on Indian affairs. This need was recognized in the U.S. Constitution with language acknowledging that various tribes of Indians were nations with which peace could be established by treaty. So from the very beginning of the life and institutions of the United States, American Indians have exerted a tenacious if tenuous presence. Now as the twentieth century ends, they comprise less than 1 percent of the population of the country, and their tenaciousness persists.

Looking selectively at the official documents that retrace the "legal" path of relations between Indians and the federal government since the pledge of "utmost good faith" in the Northwest Ordinance (1787), one might conclude that Indians have actually been dealt with generously, and that the reservation system represents the best of all possible worlds for them. But a look at other documents, and actions resulting from them, clearly reveals the pattern of conquest and betrayal that late-twentieth-century Indians point to with justifiable anger and bitter resentment.

In 1787, government policy indeed stated that "*[t]he utmost good faith shall always* be observed toward the Indians: their lands and property shall never be taken from them without their consent; and in their property, rights, and liberty, they shall never be invaded or disturbed unless in just and lawful wars" [emphasis added].

Only a few decades later, conceived under the short-lived premise that land west of the Mississippi River was uninhabitable and undesirable for white Americans, the first expression of federal removal policy occurred, in the 1817 treaty with the Cherokee Nation —a malicious, divisive maneuver from the very outset, since many Cherokee leaders opposed the decision, and only part of the tribe relocated in the designated "Indian Territory." As a result of the attempted enforcement of this treaty and others, the Office of Indian Affairs was established in 1824 as a branch of the War Department, in perhaps the most overtly honest gesture in the entire history of U.S.–Indian relations. But in 1849 the office was moved to the Department of the Interior, where it resides today.

(And here is an example of that office at work today, as recounted in a Portland *Oregonian* article published 9 December 1997: In 1990 the Bureau of Indian Affairs arranged a sale of three million board-feet of timber on the Warm Springs Reservation. According to the terms of the sale, only blown-down and wind-damaged trees were to be harvested. Instead, timber companies removed twenty-three million board-feet of timber, including healthy old-growth Noble and Douglas firs worth as much as $20,000 per tree on the export market. The U.S. Department of Justice has decided that the government was not at fault if trees were removed illegally, so the Warm Springs tribes have gone to court, asking $15 million in damages. FBI documents support claims that the Bureau of Indian Affairs badly bungled the sale.)

The reservation system evolved rapidly after the passage of the Removal Act in 1830. (In his first message to Congress in December of 1829, President Jackson had called for voluntary removal of Indians from native lands for the benefit and protection of both Indians and settlers.) Removal gained momentum, fueled by the kind of doublespeak that appears in the 1831 report of commissioner of Indian affairs Elbert Herring. Herring refers to removal as "The Humane Policy" and praises its "good effects":

> Gradually diminishing in numbers and deteriorating in condition; incapable of coping with the superior intelligence of the white man, ready to fall into vices, but inapt to appropriate the benefits of the social state; the increasing tide of white population threatened soon to engulf [the Indians], and finally to cause their total extinction. The progress is slow but sure; the cause is inherent in the nature of things; tribes numerous and powerful have disappeared from among us in a ratio of decrease, ominous to the existence of those that still remain unless counteracted by the substitution of some principle sufficiently potent to check the tendencies to decay and dissolution. This salutary principle exists in the system of removal; of change of residence; of settlement in territories exclusively their own, and under the protection of the United States; connected with

the benign influences of education and instruction in agriculture and the several mechanic arts whereby social is distinguished from savage life.

The language of this report exemplifies the prejudice and condescension that Indians faced, even though tribes were granted rights to self-government.

By the mid-1800s almost all American Indians within U.S. borders had ceased military resistance against the federal government and were living on reservations that had been established by treaty agreements. Regardless of the rhetoric implying concern for the welfare of these people, the reservation system was inarguably designed to take land from the Indians, "Americanize" or civilize the savages, and ultimately, in the process, destroy their culture and communal way of life. The General Allotment Act (1887), also known as the Dawes Act, blatantly demonstrated the federal government's intentions to break up traditional collective land use by compelling native people to accept individually deeded land parcels. The government devised its own definitions for "full blood" and "mixed blood" Indians and imposed a complex trust system. After land was allotted to every federally recognized Indian, the balance of the reservation territory was opened up to non-Indian homesteaders and other economic uses. According to Ward Churchill and Glen T. Morris in a report on key Indian laws and cases (printed in *The State of Native America*), two-thirds of all Indian land was appropriated by the government between 1887 and 1934. Under the guise of "assimilation" (Crow offering to help Eagle?), the government avidly contributed to the impoverishment of the original "Americans" and the dissolution of their social structures.

The Warm Springs Reservation, because of its remote location and its unrecognized agricultural value in the form of stands of timber, escaped being destroyed by allotment. Very few non-Indians acquired land there. By the time the Indian Reorganization Act ended allotment in 1934, the tribes of Warm Springs had developed a strong enough sense of collective identity to form their confederation and move toward true self-governance.

Yet given the legacy of the Bureau of Indian Affairs, the mandatory educational structure, and the infringement on religious freedoms that all American Indians have endured, it is useful to look once more at the Warm Springs sun box myth: When the world was moving from darkness to light, when balances were shifting, Crow stole a gift that he could neither control nor contain, and Eagle suffered a wound that hasn't yet healed.

The Seasonal Round

Life for Oregon's first inhabitants moved in a circle with the seasons, a circle that for millennia went unchanged. Time was measured by the angle and intensity of the sun, the amount of moisture in the air or soil, the number of wrinkles on an old person's face, or the size of a pregnant woman's belly. At the center of the people's existence and their imagination was the earth, with its many moods, inhabitants, and forces. The year dictated a daily and seasonal regimen, and suggested a spiritual orientation for the people. The earth gave, the people gratefully received . . .

CYNTHIA D. STOWELL, *Faces of a Reservation*

There was a dreary familiarity in these fish stories. They were part of a poisonous pattern. . . . Whether it was making electricity, irrigating the desert, or making plutonium, the pattern held: The federal government moved in on the river with urgent goals, lofty motives, and expensive machinery. It succeeded quickly, beyond anyone's expectations. It put people to work and won public approval. . . .

Then, out along the Columbia, the federal machinery quietly came under the control of narrow interests. Irrigation farmers wrote special rules that allowed them to waste water and pad their subsidies. The keepers of the plutonium factory poisoned their neighbors. Dam builders bullied, cheated, and dispossessed river Indians. And salmon died in dams.

With salmon there was something slightly different. Their decline was an event everyone witnessed, like a public hanging. Everyone who wanted to know, knew. In a region that consumed twice as much electricity per capita as the rest of the nation at rates half the national average, everyone with a light switch was a collaborator. . . .

We did it—to save on our monthly electricity bill.
BLAINE HARDEN, *A River Lost*

The Almighty took a long time to make this place.
CHIEF TOMMY THOMPSON, shortly before
Celilo Falls was drowned by The Dalles Dam

A man named Frederick K. Kramer was there when, at 10 A.M. on Sunday, 10 March 1957, the Army Corps of Engineers closed the gates of The Dalles Dam to form the pool that would drown the falls. He reports that, "Later that day I drove past Celilo. The fast water was gone, with a few rocks protruding yet above the nearly stilled waters. An ancient and historic fishery passed away and a great era on the Columbia—the great River-of-the-West— had come to an end. The Indians at Celilo with their long braids, and black, wide-brimmed hats, were watching solemnly as their heritage disappeared slowly under the water, bidding this place a silent, sad farewell." The treaty tribes were paid $27 million for the loss of Celilo, the value of the annual catch at the falls during the period 1949–1953.

"Tsagigla'lal" (as told by Wasco storyteller Brent Florendo to a Native American literature class at Southern Oregon University):

"I'm going to tell you a story of Coyote coming up the river. It's a prediction story. It shows that our people *knew* things that were coming ahead of time. This story talks about geography, geology, anthropology.

"Coyote came up the river, the Columbia River—we call it *Nch'i-Wana.* He came upon this blind man and asked him, 'Are you the leader of the village?' And the blind man said, 'No, I used to be the chief, but now there's a woman chief, and she lives up on the hill.'

"So Coyote went on way up the hill and through the village, and as he went along, he asked the people, 'Is she a good chief, or is she a bad chief?'

"And they said, 'No, she's a good chief. She teaches us how to cut our fish, and she knows when the berries are ripe and we go there; she tells us how to dig the roots and where to find them.'

"So then he goes up to where this woman chief was; her name

was Tsagigla'lal. He came to her and said, 'I hear that you're a good chief, so I'm going to do a favor for you. I'm going to turn you into a petroglyph.'

"There's a petroglyph on the Columbia called Tsagigla'lal. Our people lived in a place called Celilo Falls. It's a great waterfall on the Columbia River. It was buried behind The Dalles Dam.

"He said to her, 'This waterfall is going to go away. It's going to get buried. And the white people are going to come. And they're going to keep coming and coming and coming. And they're no longer going to let women be chiefs.

" 'But,' he said, 'things are going to come back to the way they are, and the waterfall is going to come back, and women are going to be allowed to be chiefs.'

"Now, in past history in white society, women didn't get to vote or hold corporate positions of power. My people predicted that when the white people came, women wouldn't be allowed to be chiefs anymore, but one day things would come back to the way they were before the whites came. We see that happening now. We see women's equality. We see women participating in places of power.

" 'So,' Coyote said to Tsagigla'lal, 'when everything comes back to the way it is now, you'll turn back into a human being and you'll rule the people here in this place.' "

"Native Americans"—a term not ordinarily used by those to whom it is applied—are held in fashionably high regard these days by the politically correct folks who decided a while back to call them Native Americans. Yet too many of these enlightened people, products of our technological century and therefore understandably removed from the natural world and its complex cycles, often dismiss or ignore the most crucial facets of traditional North American Indian life: hunting and fishing, and all that those pursuits meant to indigenous peoples.

Languages, dances, ceremonies, customs, religions, myths, and legends: these are the subjects commonly studied and discussed in classrooms and seminars and at conferences, and because they are the elements of life that remain on today's reservations, they are certainly very worthy subjects. But hunting, fishing, and gathering sustained tribal life through thousands of years; Indian men were warriors and dancers and storytellers occasionally, but hunters and fishers almost all the time. And, of course, Indian women performed daily functions every bit as necessary as their men's.

Now, because they come from such different roots, many white Americans are puzzled as to why Indian men and women alike are often unable or unwilling to happily accept mundane jobs (if they can find them) which will enable them to pay strangers to fulfill the daily needs that they traditionally fulfilled for themselves.

The Columbia River, which drains much of the Pacific Northwest and significant portions of the northern Rocky Mountains, has been coursing to the Pacific through the largest lava flow in North America for at least ten million years. Blades, scrapers, and bone artifacts prove that humans lived in the Celilo region at least 11,500 years ago, and salmon vertebrae discovered during excavations for The Dalles Dam indicate that the area had already become a major fishery by then.

Here, then, is how it used to be:

The Sahaptin-speaking ancestors of what are now known as the Warm Springs tribes lived in three groupings along the Columbia River. The Tenino people camped where the river narrows above The Dalles, the Wyam just above Celilo Falls near the mouth of the Deschutes, and the John Day farther east, near the mouth of the John Day River. These groups also established secondary settlements for the winter, when winds along the Columbia are often gale-force and relentless for weeks at a time. The Wascos, who spoke Chinook and were more specialized as fishermen and traders, lived below Celilo Falls and remained near the river throughout the year.

From spring through fall the salmon and steelhead runs were the central focus of activities in all the villages. Salmon and steelhead trout by the millions entered the Columbia system in early spring and ran through winter: the largest inland run of fish on earth. These fish were speared in relatively shallow water, caught with dip nets on long poles by men on rocks or scaffolding, and trapped in baskets, seine nets, and weirs. Women prepared the fish in a variety of ways: barbecuing them fresh from the streams, boiling them with roots, drying them in wind and shade for winter, and pulverizing the dried meat for trade. The bones of the first fish killed each year were ceremoniously returned to the stream to assure that the runs would continue; but of course they haven't.

In 1805 nearly three times as many salmon swam up the Columbia as there were white people living in the entire United States: about sixteen million salmon, about six million people. The estimated fifty thousand Indians then living along the Columbia took at least forty million pounds of salmon per year from the river and its tributaries—more than two pounds of fish per person per day, much to be used for trading—but this catch did nothing to diminish the huge runs.

Today, as a result of dams, pollution, logging, irrigation, and cattle grazing—as well as commercial overfishing—salmon and steelhead have been proposed for designation as endangered species in many Columbia River tributaries. Though all these listed factors have contributed significantly to the river's decline, the huge dams built for the generation of cheap power have been the major problem.

The reason the Columbia lends itself so well to power generation is that its waters fall more swiftly than those of any other North American river. The Mississippi, over its seven-hundred-mile course from St. Louis to the Gulf of Mexico, drops only a hundred feet; in four hundred miles across Washington State, the Columbia falls more than a thousand feet. The ultimate result of this circumstance is summed up succinctly in a quotation from Al Wright of the Pacific Northwest Utilities Conference Committee: "We took a pristine river and we turned it into a working river—a machine. And it is a damn fine machine."

The dams are there, almost surely immovable and permanent, and the machine river, as author Blaine Hardin calls it, goes about its twentieth-century economic business; but the fish runs could be at least partially restored if only other more solvable problems were addressed in time. Unfortunately, though, there seems to be little reason for optimism.

In 1997, with the endorsement of the Warm Springs Tribal Council, a small, very determined group of Oregonians coordinated by a young woman named Ashley Henry collected enough signatures to get a "Clean Streams" initiative on the state ballot. This initiative would have required ranchers to fence cattle away from streams on their ranches—streams that have been devastated by overgrazing, trampled vegetation, and the annual deposit of thousands of tons of excrement. During the campaign leading up to the vote, ranchers outspent initiative backers by at least twenty to one, most of their money going toward misleading print and television advertisements. Governor John Kitzhaber, an avowed environmentalist, refused to support the measure. Instead, he sided with the ranchers, who promised to work with him privately to solve the problem—a promise that, once the measure was defeated, they never fulfilled.

In the fall of 1996 the Columbia River Inter-Tribal Fish Commission wrote to Governor Kitzhaber and to the Clinton administration (one of many such letters) asking that steps be taken to restore the runs. Accompanying the letter were seventy photographs of the stream banks in the John Day and Grand Ronde watersheds, where the silt on the spawning beds, caused exclusively by overgrazing, is so thick that virtually no salmon or steelhead survive. So far, as usual, nothing has been done to improve the situation.

Occasionally a practical environmental opportunity presents itself, and when it does, the Warm Springs tribes respond. On 20 October 1999, the Portland *Oregonian* reported the $5.6 million purchase of a thirty-thousand-acre ranch in Wheeler County by the Confederated Tribes. The purchase was made possible by funds from the Bonneville Power Administration, which is required by Congress to compensate the public for wildlife habitat destroyed by the construction of the Columbia River dams. The Pine Creek Ranch contains one of only four John Day River tributaries where threatened wild summer steelhead continue to spawn, and the tribes' principal aim will be to protect this spawning habitat and to boost populations of other endemic wildlife species, such as elk and antelope, as well.

Unfortunately, though, neither federal nor state bureaucracies are often receptive to Indians' (or anyone else's) complaints or pleas, so most battles to save salmon and steelhead are fought in the courts these days, by the Warm Springs people as well as the Yakamas, Umatillas, and Nez Percé. From the 1940s through the 1960s, the federal government paid very little attention to Indian grievances as the huge dams were constructed one after another on both the Columbia and its major tributary, the Snake. Finally, with the completion of Grand Coulee Dam on the Columbia and Hells Canyon on the Snake, neither with fish ladders, one-third of the river system simply became closed forever to migrating fish.

More than any other single factor, the subsequent sharp decline in the runs led to the tribes' reliance on legal actions, and they have subsequently won several important court cases: In 1969 U.S. District Judge Robert Belloni ruled that states could not regulate fishing by Indians who had treaty rights and that Indians indeed had a claim to a fair share of the fish; then, in 1974, U.S. District Judge George Boldt ruled that 50 percent of the harvestable runs constituted a fair share. Both of these decisions were based on the treaties of 1855, which ceded Indian lands in exchange for reservation lands and the right to continue fishing in "usual and accustomed places."

The Columbia Inter-Tribal Fish Commission was established in 1977 to represent the fishing rights of the four treaty tribes. As the commission's recent complaint to Governor Kitzhaber and President Clinton clearly indicates, salmon allocations mean very little if the fish runs continue to disappear; so restoring the runs, rather than dividing them up, has become the major issue. At one commission meeting an Indian suggested discussion on how the last surviving salmon to enter the river system should be carved into pieces and distributed; another perhaps less practical man suggested blowing up the Columbia system dams so that Celilo and other flooded falls could roar once again. (By 1999 some environmentalists, and even a few politicians, were talking about the possibility of breaching some Columbia River system dams; but the chances of this ever happening must be considered extremely remote.)

By May 1997, the Inter-Tribal Commission had become so disillusioned with the situation that it angrily withdrew from the Columbia and Snake Rivers salmon restoration and review process. Ted Strong, the commission's executive director, stated the reason succinctly: "We find the decisions are not being made for the salmon. The decisions are being made in the defense of the federal hydropower system that has been developed on the Columbia River."

In January of 1999, after literally thousands of hours of discussion and argument, the northwest states, eleven Indian tribes, and six federal agencies finally agreed to create a panel to save Columbia River salmon.

Then, on 16 March 1999, the National Marine Fisheries Service listed nine salmon and steelhead populations in Washington and Oregon for protection under the federal Endangered Species Act. Ted Strong's reactions to these developments were published on 28 March 1999 in the Portland *Oregonian:*

> *We counted on technology to fix problems at the dams. But those approaches have proven to be a bust. We have tried to repair and restore damaged habitat. But habitat destruction has continued far faster than we can keep up with, much less overcome it. The parties to the Columbia River Fish Management Plan have refused to follow through on their promises to rebuild upriver salmon, leaving naturally spawning salmon weaker than ever.*
>
> *Perhaps saddest, most disappointing of all, is how the federal government has used the Endangered Species Act as leverage, not to protect and restore salmon, but to protect and enrich the industries that benefit from the very things that have caused the demise of salmon. Justified by its "biological opinion," the federal government continues to rely heavily on putting juvenile salmon in trucks and barges, even though it isn't working. More screens, bigger screens are added in front of the turbines as part of elaborate bypass systems under the auspices of the Endangered Species Act, even though there is mounting evidence that these systems are doing more harm than good. It becomes more and more obvious that what passes for science is being used not as a means to pursue truth but to justify what is politically expedient.*
>
> *At the same time, the federal government sharply attacks tribal harvest, not only commercial, but also ceremonial and subsistence, even though eliminating tribal harvest altogether won't come close to stopping the slide of Columbia Basin salmon toward extinction. I see it as part of the withering attacks upon their sovereignty that tribal governments have had to withstand. But I put my faith in the tribes. Only if tribal people hold*

on to their timeless and priceless customs will salmon be protected. They are the salmon's last line of defense, last hedge against extinction. . . . My heart and mind will always be on the side where salmon are being loved and honored.

Memories of Celilo Falls remain a powerful force at Warm Springs. In the rather lavish dining room at Kah-Nee-Ta Lodge, an entire wall—the only entire wall in the large room—is decorated with dip nets, carved fish, and large framed photographs of the fishing at the falls showing the men perched on their scaffolding, ropes around their waists for safety, the white water churning and thundering below them. Upstairs in the lodge, a similar set of photographs lines the long hallway that leads to tribal offices. All of these photographs (some of them for sale at the lodge gift shop) date from 1956, the year before The Dalles Dam was completed.

Down the road at the Warm Springs Museum, a short orientation film is shown to visitors, and it too features Celilo, with the big Chinook salmon, like living arrows, leaping into the white water as they fight their way toward spawning. Water, the film's narrator tells us, is sacred to local tribes, as are the big, gleaming fish. At a recent tribal art exhibit in the museum, by far the largest painting on display was an acrylic rendering of Celilo Falls by Susana Santos, who, in her "artist's statement," described herself as a "traditional fisherwoman."

In various university libraries in Oregon, a twenty-two-and-a-half-minute video produced by a man named William Cole is available. Titled "Last Days at Celilo," it treats the subject, no doubt without conscious ill will, from the viewpoint of the white culture. Well over half of the video deals with the construction of an eight-and-a-half-mile canal, begun in 1903 and completed in 1915, that was dug around Celilo Falls to accommodate steamboat traffic. Nothing about the falls or the river or fish is described as sacred or holy; instead, everything is quantified. A typical example is the narrator's solemn listing of equipment on hand at the close of 1910: "four steam shovels, one land dredge, fifteen locomotives, eighty-three dump cars, one rock crusher, one sand grinding plant, two concrete mixing plants, two air compressor plants, thirty steam and air drills, one electric light plant, and thirty-one horses. . . . [T]he excavation totaled 1,402,000 yards of rock and 1,606,000 yards of sand.... [N]o records were kept of the number of men killed while completing the project." When the subject shifts, finally, to the traditional Indian fishing at Celilo Falls, the unfortunate viewpoint remains consistent: the narrator reads us a catalogue of various dip-netting techniques, an account of tons of fish caught, canned, and consumed, and the fluctuations in the price per pound for salmon in different years. Finally, the video concludes with this rather impressive monument to insensitive understatement: "It was a sad experience for some when the gates at The Dalles Dam were dropped on a Sunday morning in March 1957, and the fishing sites and fast water of the river were inundated by the rising pool behind that project."

When the falls roared and the salmon ran as they were meant to, all of the Warm Springs groups acted as middlemen in a trade network that extended west to the Pacific, north into Canada, east as far as the Rocky Mountains, and south all the way to California. Dried salmon was traded for shells and roots from the west; baskets, beads, and blankets from the north; horses and buffalo hides from the east; and feathers, baskets, obsidian, and bows and arrows from the south.

While the Wascos lived by the river throughout the year, the Sahaptins traveled widely to gather edible flowers, roots, and berries. Bitterroot and balsamroot could be dug from early spring through June, followed by Indian potato and camas. In late summer, huckleberries ripened in the mountains, chokecherries near the streams. While the women dug cedar roots to make bags, nets, and clothing, and picked black lichen from the firs and pines to pit roast, the men hunted deer and elk, as well as smaller game. The women smoked the meat and made thread from sinew, needles and fishhooks from bones, and tools from antlers. Skins of wolf, coyote, bear, cougar, otter, beaver, raccoon, and rabbit were taken for use as household items and for trade.

During the fall, cattails and tule reeds were harvested from river banks to use in constructing mat-covered shelters. As winter approached, summer villages were dismantled, firewood was collected and stored, and the winter villages were built in their sheltered sites away from the river.

Through the winter months, there was limited hunting and stream fishing when weather and conditions allowed. Tools, weapons, clothing, and household items were fashioned: canoes, digging sticks, arrow and spear shafts, fire drills, dip net hoops, snowshoes, and cradle boards.

Storytelling for both entertainment and instruction was a central activity in all the winter villages. By late March, as days lengthened and warmed, winter villages were dismantled in their turn, and back at the big river, high now with snow melt, the fish runs and seasonal round commenced once again.

The shifting boundary that the Wascos and Warm Springs tribes shared with the Northern Paiutes was in the area occupied by the Warm Springs Reservation today. Though they utilized some of the same foods as their river neighbors, the Paiutes had their own language—a Uto-Aztecan tongue that linked them with both the Hopi of the Southwest and the Aztecs of Mexico—and their own distinct cultural traditions. It would probably be exaggeration to claim that the Paiutes warred with their neighbors, but disagreements and skirmishes were fairly common. It is also likely that antagonisms between the tribes increased during the nineteenth century, due to pressure from a rapidly growing population of whites forcing the Paiutes north and the river people south.

The dry, rocky lands of what is now eastern Oregon didn't provide an easy life. The Paiutes did without an abundance of salmon and weren't involved with the lucrative trading activity on the Columbia. Roots, seeds, and game were major food sources. In the spring, with streams high and lakes full, they used small boats of tule reeds or wooden dugouts to collect edible plants and hunt waterfowl with the help of tule decoys. Rainbow and cutthroat trout, suckers, and a few salmon were taken in willow traps or with spears.

When summer's intense heat arrived, families went their separate ways to harvest berries, seeds, small game, and even insects.

Fall, another period of relative plenty, produced the largest communal gatherings of the yearly cycle. Hunting was primarily for deer and antelope, and more seeds and nuts were collected, much of the food dried for winter use.

By November the dried foods were carried to winter camps near water. Winter homes were domed willow frames covered with tule mats, cattail, or sagebrush, and placed where they were sheltered from the worst weather. Groups of families often wintered together and shared with each other and with nearby camps if anyone ran short of provisions. The cold months were a time for telling stories and making tools and household items: utensils, clothing, juniper bows, berry wood arrows with obsidian points, axes, and clubs.

Because they covered so much ground to satisfy their needs, the extended family was the most practical grouping through most of the year. Temporary leaders were sometimes chosen in spring and fall when specific circumstances required it. Because of their difficult lives, the Paiutes were tough and resourceful people.

In *The Hungry Summer* (Barrow, Alaska: North Slope Borough Planning Department, 1989), author John M. Campbell comments succinctly on the sort of life the Paiutes lived: "It is nearly impossible for modern man to imagine what it is like to live by hunting. The life of a hunter is one of hard, seeming continuous overland travel . . . [and] of frequent concerns that the next interception may not work, that the trap or the drive will fail, or that the herds will not appear this season. Above all, the life of a hunter carries with it the threat of deprivation and death by starvation."

These seasonal rounds weren't merely practical necessities; they were education in the truest, deepest sense of the word: education through life process, not merely the conventional passing-on of information usually practiced in schoolrooms today. Tracking and stalking a deer or elk or antelope, killing cleanly, butchering the animal efficiently, then skinning it; dipping a thrashing sixty-pound Chinook salmon from a roaring river with a small net at the end of a long, limber pole—all of this demanded the mastery of exceedingly difficult skills. Strength, endurance, and coordination were required, along with deep knowledge of complex natural cycles. Beadwork, tanning hides, weaving, basketry, and toolmaking—these taught patience and dexterity and, even more importantly, created in every individual who contributed a strong and unquestioned sense of purpose.

Obviously, life was often challenging and sometimes dangerous.

There were floods and blizzards, earthquakes and volcanic eruptions; and the hard times inevitably taught cooperation. When survival is at stake, people get along.

But now, as far as any opportunity for the preservation of traditional life is concerned, American Indians, the Confederate Tribes of the Warm Springs included, are restricted to their reservations. What have they lost? Land, certainly, and many sacred places like Celilo Falls; the freedom that went with the old life; many of the skills that made life possible, and the lessons these skills taught — and even more.

Here are some pertinent words of Peter John, an Athabasca who was eighty-two years old when interviewed by *Gray's Sporting Journal* (Winter 1982, Vol. 7, No. 1: 78) in Alaska in 1982:

> *Life is — if you live good and take care of yourself — the body is just like a machine and if you take care of your body it's going to stand up. We never had disease because people don't stay one place all the time — move. They move to new place, clean place. They go out hunting, don't stay overnight where there's people been before. We camp out where there's clean place, nice ground, no germs. That's the way people used to live long time ago. So very seldom you get sick. Never seen no people was sick when I was kid, except maybe cold sometimes, but that's all. And I see more people ninety, hundred years old, snowshoe all day and never even feel it. So that's the kind of people that used to live long time ago. There is nothing that they can't do. One Indian I hears of run eighty miles one day. Clubbed fox with stick. His name Chitahaus.*
>
> *Those Indians that I seen, they could tell what kind of bear just by looking at the den. They can tell. Just by looking at the moose track they can tell what kind of moose. So we're talking about people that really understand and when them people that used to use bow and arrow long time ago — the arrow would just go right through the body. We see weak Indians right now. Too weak.*

The depressing rates among twentieth-century American Indians of such diseases as alcoholism and diabetes are well known and widely documented. There have been no medical studies to explain these diseases among Indian populations, but simple logic would seem to explain them clearly enough. When people live for countless generations on wild meat and native plant life, their bodies are bound to suffer from sudden infusions of sugar, salt, and lard, not to mention alcohol.

American Indians had no more resistance to many of our foods than they did to small pox and measles, and the fact that they continue to suffer because of this should come as no surprise to anybody. As Peter John tells us, the people used to hunt and move and they were strong; and now they live in one place, with canned food and Budweiser beer, electric stoves and refrigerators, tools from Sears and clothes from Wal-Mart.

So the seasonal round has vanished forever; the Columbia River has been transformed into a series of sluggish, muddy reservoirs. But on the Warm Springs Reservation now, the people struggle to keep their traditional culture alive, and that becomes our subject.

Brent Florendo

Brent grew up on the Warm Springs Reservation and is currently enrolled as a theater arts major at Southern Oregon University in Ashland. In his forties, he lives in town with his wife and daughter. He is a good-looking man with a strong, compact build that once served him well as a competitive wrestler. His mother was Wasco; his father, Filipino.

The salmon runs are about shot. I had some friends that were down at Sherars Bridge about a week ago. They opened it for a little while to hook-and-line fishing, but they weren't getting any. I talked to my brother-in-law yesterday, and I think they closed it back down again. They usually give you one shot, and if you're lucky, you catch fish. It's pretty much shot. Our tribe is one of the first tribes that said we're not going to fish. We shut ourselves down before anybody else did, and then a few other tribes followed suit.

My folks had a place on the Deschutes River, and it used to be really nice when I was a kid. But anymore in the summertime, like now, they start floating down at daybreak, four o'clock in the morning, and they're floating by till it gets dark, one after another, after another. Trout fishing is still pretty good considering the traffic, but the salmon left are hatchery salmon. The fight they have over what's left I think's a joke. My understandings are that the allocations to the Indians are so far behind what they owe us. We should have all the fish that're left. I think we're supposed to be allowed half the amount, and every year we never get it. It's hard to get salmon anymore. It's really, really hard to get salmon. Like for our powwow here, I used to call home to Warm Springs and say,

Brent Florendo (AUTHOR PHOTO)

"Hey, we're having a powwow," and I'd get two hundred pounds of salmon—they'd do it just like that. Now they only give salmon out for funerals and real special dinners. Sometimes weddings, but mostly funerals.

In two, two and a half years I should get my bachelor of fine arts in acting and directing. I'd prefer to stay here in the area after that. A lot of people say you have to run off to LA or New York. The thing I want to do besides acting is write for the stage, and I'd like to write contemporary Native American themes. Not many people are doing that now; there are only a couple of Native American companies, so the theater world is wide open. What's out there now always seems to reflect back into our cultural past, for the most part. The only way the masses seem to be able to identify with us is in the past. My idea is: We're still here; we're a viable people; we have the same heartbreaks, the same successes, the same failures as everybody else does. Besides that, I think we have our own humor and goals, our own priorities, our own principles that are unique to Native American people. Some of them are sad; some of them are happy; but I think that the tension that happens with Native American people is something that could be presented on stage in a tasteful manner for entertainment, for education, and for the sheer fact that we need to be recognized as a people. We're here yet, but it's like we're invisible, and it seems like it's always kind of been that way. An individual can go off and stand out, and people say, "He's a Native American," but people as a whole don't recognize all of us that same way, and I think that the stage is a perfect place to do that.

I was raised on the reservation. They have an elementary school on the reservation, and when you get to junior high and high school, you go to Madras, about fifteen miles away. There used to be a lot of racism, but Madras has changed considerably. The Chicano population is immense there now. Now there's a new animosity between the Mexicans and the Indians, mostly gangs, the young people. I think the teachers have a double standard. In athletics, sometimes the Indian kids have more talent, but the white kids get on the team. There are so many outrageously gifted athletic kids on the reservation. A lot of kids get lost, fall through the cracks. The racism has always been there, and I think it'll always be there until our people make another stand.

I've been to four different schools. When I first started out, a lot of the guidance and counseling I was taken into wasn't really anything that fulfilled what my dreams were. They were just kind of geared toward, "This is what you're capable of doing."

I was a good wrestler at Madras. Athletics kept me in school, and I got really good grades, and then dislocated my arm when I was a sophomore. I knew I was never going to get to wrestle again at the level I was at; there was just no way. When I did wrestle, the longer my hair got, the less my coach talked to me. That really broke my spirit, because I was really naive. In my sophomore year I got most valuable wrestler—I was good. I finally realized I was the one making my coach look good. I didn't know how good I was; I was just going from one tournament to the next, and I just happened to keep winning. When I saw what was happening, it really broke my spirit—to see that this man I put my whole trust into, to see that I wasn't a person to him; I was a thing, and I was useful to him. I kind of crashed after that. My whole junior year was a mess. I started skipping school and partying and running off. I never graduated, but passed my GED and went to Lane Community College. I just wanted *out.*

I went to Lane Community College, but I didn't fare there very well. I'd do real well for about half a term, but the whole newness of the place—the transition wasn't smooth; there wasn't a big support group. My inability to talk to non-native students in the school working on projects and things like that held me back. I dropped out, and I'd start again and drop out.

Then I went to Alaska. I told myself the best move for me was to get away from the reservation, and I went to Alaska. Everybody thought I'd be back in a year or two, but one thing led to another. I enrolled at the University of Alaska and met some people up there and started singing. That's when I really started in the theater world. I sang in the civic opera in Alaska when it first started, the first couple years. Never in my wildest dreams do I think I'd have ever had an opportunity to sing in an opera company here in Oregon. It just wouldn't have happened. There's no way in hell it would have happened. There were people up there that thought I had talent. I even coached wrestling up there, and there's no way in hell I'd ever get to coach wrestling in Madras as an Indian. Going to Alaska helped me build my self-esteem, because I was on my own up there. That's what launched me to where I am today.

I've learned this from being off the reservation working for different people. We need to teach our kids—I think it's a new trend— we need to try to talk our kids into leaving the reservation and staying away long enough to gain experience from the best people. Once you gain that experience, you have the knowledge to go back to the reservation and say, "Okay, now I've brought the whole package back, not just myself."

I'd love to go home to the Warm Springs Reservation. I've told them, "Build an amphitheater here." It's a natural place for that, and we could build a whole new clientele of people coming to our resort. It's not that far from Portland [100 miles], and we could do this.

I don't have any problem with my daughter growing up off the reservation, because I think that I've made the transition. I'm able to explain how to get back to the reservation. What I had to do to get off it I can reverse and tell her how to get back.

I talk in the analogy of the bridge. Everybody says you have to live in two worlds all the time. Well, in these two worlds there's a bridge, and a foundation has to be established on each side for the bridge to be viable. This is the reservation foundation; this is the off-the-reservation foundation [motions with his hands]. Why do we have this bridge? So that our children can cross over to whichever side of the bridge they need to in order to succeed. Not everybody's made to live on the reservation, and not everybody's made to live off the reservation. But the thing that used to happen between these two things, there used to be an animosity that flowed between these two foundations and made it weak. If I go back now and voice my opinion about the politics, maybe somebody's going to say to me, "You don't have any right, because you don't live here." But if people out here don't bring back the knowledge of how to run our administration, how to run our resort, how to run our environment, all these things that you learn out here that are white man's ways. So they have to count on me to help by bringing that information back. So what do I get out of it if I live my life off the reservation, as a lot of urban Indians do? What are urban Indians looking for? They're looking for "How do I learn to drum, how do I learn to dance, where are my roots? How do I make a choker?" Our old people still know how to cut meat right, dry deer meat the old way, tan hides. When I come back, I count on them to have kept those things for me. That's what I get. If they can keep that for me I'll do this for them. But there can't be any animosity between the two sides.

I think the success lies in how good a tie did I keep with my friends back home. What kind of respect do they have for me, even if I've been gone to Alaska, even though I'm down here going to school? Did I remember where I came from? When I went home to the reservation, did I go down to the Rainbow Market and buy a case of beer and invite everybody down to the river and go drink beer with them? I'm a sociable drinker; I can go drink beer; but to them, it was the start of a three-day weekend. But did I still do that, or did I say, "No, you guys are bad examples; I can't do that"? No, that's my people, for God's sake. I understand why they're doing that—it's because they don't have anything better to do—but that doesn't mean that they're not good people.

If I come back and act judgmental, they're going to say, "Screw you; you're not one of us anymore." But if I remember where I came from all my life, I can relate to these people, and they can identify with me. Now when I go home, people want to know what I have to say. They want to know what my opinions are. They respect me, and I respect them.

That's the bridge back to the reservation. Remember I said that I thought our kids had to start leaving the reservation? Well, they need to leave to someplace where there's somebody like me sitting out here that knows where they're coming from, that has respect. Their parents can say, "Go ahead and go out there, because I trust that man out there that I'm sending you to." Then the kids have a choice. They can go back and forth across this bridge as they need to, when they need to, and be able to literally live in both worlds.

You asked about my daughter. I have a strong energy line back to home and what my parents taught me, and my elders, and I'll have that to give to my daughter.

When I was a young man, my mom was very progressive. She was the first Businesswoman of the Year in Oregon—the first woman that ever got that award—and an Indian woman on top of that. She was in the forefront, and that's the way we were raised.

I fought the first ten years of my life on the reservation because I was a half-breed and because we had money, because both my parents worked. We had things.

Old people would want to give me Indian outfits, and my mom said, "No, I don't want him involved in that yet. He's got to go learn to read, write, do arithmetic, and be twice as good at it just because his skin's brown." That's the way it had been for her. So she didn't allow me to Indian dance. She told me if I ever really wanted to dance in my heart, I would pursue it, and I did. I didn't start dancing until I was thirteen years old, and I've been a fancy dancer ever since. I'm accepted anywhere I go, and people recognize me as a fancy dancer, legit, all the way. I did the contest thing; I did the circuit, did it all.

Well, that's the same thing I feel about my daughter. I'll teach her all the things that I know, and I'll take her home at times. There will be times we go to huckleberry feasts, salmon feasts, go to funerals, and she'll sit and watch me take part in a funeral, and I'll explain to her what my reasons are and why I'm doing this. This transition has happened for me this past year, when both my folks passed away. I had a nephew, an uncle, and both my parents pass away, elders in our family, and I had to step up to the next level and do things that I used to just sit and watch.

My wife is a Cherokee from North Carolina. She's been gone from there for a number of years. I've never been there, but I hope to maybe get over there in late August, right before school starts in the fall, go over for a couple of weeks. I got to get over there and dance. I've dreamed about it a couple of times. I dreamed about dancing for her family, all of her family over there, and I intend to make it over there and do that.

Our reservation has every type of terrain that's available in the state of Oregon. The reservation line's Mount Jefferson—we own half of Mount Jeff—so it's clear up to alpine and down into the Deschutes River canyon. It's the best back yard any kid could have. I spent a lot of time out in it. Whenever I wasn't doing sports, I was out in it fishing or hunting. Our whole family would go fishing

Brent Florendo

every weekend. We'd meet another family, and that was our family thing we did.

I've had black people tell me, "Why don't you have your senators, why don't you have your mayors?" It's because our people don't choose to make their way through this world that way. You decided to become part of the system; we don't. We want to keep our identity; that's the way I look at it. Even if we got our 1 percent of the population, got them all to vote on the same idea, what good would it do?

We take responsibility for raising ourselves up to become better people in a positive way, not to be radical or to be racist toward white people. The white tribe needs to educate themselves about Indian people too. They're the ones that put us in this position a long time ago. Sometimes when I talk about this in a class, the proverbial white kid in the corner speaks up and says, "Well, I wasn't back there when that happened." I hate that; it drives me nuts. I could jump on it, but I don't do that anymore. I know how to say things that aren't really pleasant to hear, but I can say it in such a way that it's just a fact. I can say, "Let's look at it this way. This is what's happening now, and it's still reflective of the same thing that happened back then. Maybe you weren't there doing that, but this is what you're doing now. You're a part of this thing that's happening right here today." Some other Indian guy could come in there and say the same thing, and he'd just be so damn militant and he'd have everybody in an uproar, and it wouldn't serve any purpose whatsoever except to piss somebody off. I want to make a positive impact.

I had to go do research up here in this library, and I was in the Native American section looking around, and I got to looking at all these tribes, and I saw a couple of my own people. I opened books and looked for Wasco and found bits and pieces. I'd see books and realize, "My mom's in this." It's an eerie feeling to open a book and read something my mom said, find pictures of her, acknowledgments about her. She worked with Dr. French, the anthropologist. She helped do the world phonetic language, get our language known in the world. She helped do that. That's what kind of person she was. She moved even into the library; she'll be there for-ever. Many libraries, all over the world, she can be in. But the feel-ing I had, standing inside of those books, was overwhelming. I sat down; I just literally sat down and looked at them all and thought about how many Indian people are in these books. Where'd they go? Where's their families now? Where are those people? What's happened to them?

One Thousand Square Miles

You know our treaty guarantees we can fish in all the usual and
accustomed places. Well, they took away some of the best places when
they built the Bonneville Dam and flooded them. They promised to
give us four hundred acres in lieu sites, but more than fifty years
later, we still got only forty. When they built The Dalles Dam,
drowning Celilo Falls, we got rooked on that deal, too. Not to
mention Hanford and all the radio-active crap it's dumping in our
river. Over the years, a lot of our people been pushed off the river,
and they're still trying to push us . . .

Now you know some of our people have been put in prison
lately for fishing, even though that's what the Creator wants them
to do. But that white man's law is no good for people . . . who
understand the river and the old laws. We got a treaty that says
we're a sovereign nation.

CRAIG LESLEY, *River Song*

A map of the state of Oregon (96,981 square miles) appears on an
atlas page as an irregular rectangle. In the northwestern quarter
of this rectangle is a small and irregular square (about 1,000 square
miles) which constitutes the Warm Springs Reservation. In a spirit
of obvious symbolism, color the reservation red and the rest of the
state white. As a visual aid, this will serve to adequately suggest
the relative size and power of two very different cultures, and to
demonstrate why many of the people of Warm Springs are acutely
conscious of being quite literally surrounded. To look at it another
way, the people who live in the white portion of the map can easily
ignore the small red square if they choose to; but for those who live
inside the square, the huge, encompassing whiteness is a constant
presence.

A few days and nights spent near the border between the two worlds, talking and listening, can reveal a good deal about the way some local whites regard Warm Springs Indians. Ordinary racists, who exist wherever there are sizable ethnic minorities and whose insults and epithets are depressingly predictable, contribute no more than a rudimentary beginning to an understanding of the feuds and animosities that matter here; but, though their viewpoint is myopic, the generic racists need to be heard.

To an occasional visitor, most rural Oregon taverns look and feel about the same. Always there is a juke box with a selection made up primarily, if not exclusively, of country-western songs and a glaring neon sign advertising Budweiser, Miller, or Coors. Usually there is at least one coin-operated pool table, sometimes a shuffle-board machine instead, and, increasingly, a lineup of video poker games subsidized by the state lottery board (machines that blink, beep, whine, and ring and devour hard-earned dollar bills at an alarming rate). As often as not, large jars of deviled eggs and spiced Polish sausages sit near the cash register, and it's never a surprise to find a crude joke, printed as a poster, displayed on a wall or the mirror behind the bar: for example, SEX INSTRUCTIONS GIVEN HERE: FIRST LESSON FREE. The lighting is on the dark side, and the stale air smells of cigarette smoke, the rancidness increasing with the hour.

Most of the customers are working men, or retired working men, many of them with lady friends or wives, who undoubtedly confer a civilizing influence with their presence.

Topics of conversation are no more varied than decor or clientele: work, money, politics, sports, guns, hunting, fishing, and, in the Warm Springs area, Indians. Along with environmentalists, Indians are usually reviled. Most of this sort of talk occurs fairly late in the evenings, when beer has loosened tongues and clouded minds.

In just such a place, between ten and eleven in the evening on a Friday, Del and his wife Ella, along with Bart and his wife (whose name was never mentioned), all of whom look to be in their forties, sat in an upholstered booth.

The heavyset men wore jeans and western shirts; the pale

women, printed dresses. On their Formica table sat two large pitchers of draft beer, four glasses, two piles of money anchored down by change, an opened pack of Marlboros, and an ashtray nearly full of filter-tipped butts, at least half of them with lipstick stains.

Their booth was separated from the bar by a pool table where two-man teams, loggers by their dress, shot games of eight-ball badly and often cursed loudly at missed shots. Juke box music played continuously, but not so loudly that the conversation couldn't be overheard from the next row of booths: a conversation, it turned out, that might have comfortably included Huck Finn's Pap.

The subject of Indians came up when Del asked Ella how much she'd spent that day on her grocery shopping.

ELLA: Eighty-three, eighty-four dollars.

DEL: What?

ELLA: Eighty-three, eighty-four dollars is what.

DEL: What the hell'd you buy? Lobsters? Goddamn champagne and caviar?

ELLA: I bought what I always buy is all.

BART'S WIFE: If these guys went and shopped themselves, maybe then they'd know how it is, Ella.

ELLA: Don't go betting on that. You know what frosted my ass?

BART: Watch that mouth, woman.

DEL: Shit, you ought to hear her at home.

ELLA: Out in the lot when the boy loaded my groceries in, some Indian was parked right there next door in a brand new shiny pickup truck.

DEL: Brand new?

ELLA: *Brand* new. Shiny red. It still had that sticker thing from the show room on the window.

BART: What kind of Indian was it?

BART'S WIFE: How many kinds are there?

BART: Well, there's young ones and old ones, big ones and little ones. Men and women, I guess.

DEL: An' drunk ones, don't forget.

BART: That's pretty near all of 'em, ain't it?

ELLA: Well this one was a young one, a kid almost, maybe twenty. Sometimes it's hard to tell with them. He loaded enough groceries in that thing to feed a whole tribe for about a month, too.

DEL: All they do on that reservation is freeload off the government. That's *my* opinion.

BART'S WIFE: They got a resort, and that casino. Remember, we saw it once. They got a lumber mill too, don't they?

DEL: An' they got it all off the damn government!

BART: You got that right!

ELLA: We ain't got any brand new pickup truck, any shiny red one, an' I guarantee you we never will.

Several seconds of silence.

BART: Where you gonna hunt this year?

DEL: Deer?

BART: Elk.

DEL: Over around La Grande, with Shorty. You?

BART: I ain't huntin' elk. Where you huntin' deer?

DEL: Up by Maupin maybe. You?

BART: I ain't huntin' deer either.

BART'S WIFE: What he means is, Del, when you go out around 2 A.M. with a spotlight; usually they don't call it huntin'.

Laughter all around.

BART: Where I'd *like* to hunt would be on that reservation.

DEL: Yeah, well, those Indians sneak out on our land and shoot whatever the hell they feel like whenever they want. But don't you get caught on their land, or your white ass's in some deep trouble.

BART: Down at Oscar's the other day—I went to buy bait—I saw a Mex buyin' a huntin' license an' a deer tag. He talked like—you remember, that Speedy guy, that mouse on the cartoons—when he talked.

DEL: You see anything and everything these days. My brother saw—this was in June I guess—he saw a nigger in a drift boat down on the Deschutes.

BART: In a drift boat?

DEL: With a white damn guide no less. Trout fishin'. *Fly* fishin'.

BART: Really?

DEL: He saw it, and he ain't blind.

BART: I bet he was on some pro team. Had to be.

Abruptly, the topic became the likely fates of the Seattle Seahawks and the San Francisco 49ers during the coming professional football season; the draft beer and the racial talk continued to flow. Del and Bart counted themselves Seahawk fans. "You wait!" Bart said at one point. "Their niggers'll beat our niggers again this year!"

Opinions of relatively well intentioned whites exemplify some of the complex tensions at play between the two cultures.

The men quoted at length below were willing to talk, but only with a promise of anonymity. Given what they had to say, that seemed reasonable. Both men gave distinct impressions of sincerity and honesty; and it is precisely these qualities that prove how wide the gulf between the white and Indian worlds remains.

The Rainbow Market is a kind of Warm Springs landmark. Only a few yards removed from the eastern bank of the Deschutes, which forms the eastern border of the reservation, it sells groceries, beer, clothing, and fishing permits. On a midmorning in July, only six or eight cars and pickups are parked outside in the expansive lot. In the last vehicle in line, a blue Ford Bronco, a former Madras politician and lifelong resident of the area tells of his impressions of the reservation:

"Most of the settlers who came here in the old days weren't bad people—unfortunately, plenty of them were, though. When you start talking in terms of racism, it is a terrible, terrible thing. I've experienced it too. A good number of people on the reservation dislike white people. I've lived with it for many years. At one time I thought maybe that I could make a difference. But I couldn't.

"I'll tell you the ugly truth. It isn't very pleasant, but I'll do it. The problems they have are so ingrained. It starts with their leadership. One of their former bigwigs committed at least thirty criminal acts. He should be in prison. He's stolen from the tribe, victimized them for years. Some of the people who have been on the Tribal Council—you couldn't believe it. But when they try to prosecute somebody, it doesn't ever work. Hardly anybody ever gets convicted."

A middle-aged Indian parks nearby in a Chevrolet so old that the paint is peeling off the body in strips. He walks into the market with a black plastic trash bag

Downtown Madras (AUTHOR PHOTO)

bulging with aluminum cans, while his wife and young son wait in the car. Just as
he passes through the door, two Indian men come out carrying quarts of beer and
discussing the merits of various brands of house paint.

"The problem is, the tribe has its own justice system, with all
kinds of hoops to jump through. There are maybe a dozen or more
major crimes — the murders and rapes and really serious things —
that are handled federally. There's a BIA investigator that handles
most of the serious crimes on the reservation, these really serious
felony crimes. But the problem is, things that, off the reservation,
would be treated as a felony crime, on the reservation normally are
not. The attitude of the federal government or the BIA is a sort of
hands-off approach. It's their reservation, their people, and they
have their own police department and their own justice system, so,
if possible, let them handle it. So they end up leaving an awful lot
of things within the tribal system that shouldn't be within that
system. It happens far too often. There's people over there who are
drug dealers, rapists, murderers, the lowest form of human beings
walking around. Would this happen in Madras? Would people like
this be walking around? The chance is zero. Absolute zero.

"The reason bad people can sometimes get elected to the Tribal
Council is they have enough family members in their districts
to get elected. Family members that have problems want people
they're related to on the Tribal Council. Some of the voting dis-

tricts are so small; a family and their friends can pretty much win in any election they want.

"The good people should be the ones running the tribe—and there's a bunch of them over there that are just outstanding individuals, hard-working people with morals and a lot of ambition, aggressive people. Some of these folks are wealthy because of the timber industry. There's ways for those people to succeed, and some of them do. But these successful people usually don't get involved in any way with tribal government. They have plenty of money, they have good kids, and they just don't want to be involved in this kind of situation. They don't need it."

A young Indian in a rusty Pontiac rolls slowly through the parking lot, car windows wide open, rap music pounding loudly and relentlessly, as an elderly Indian woman in a wheelchair talks on the outdoor public telephone. As the Pontiac passes, the woman presses a hand to her ear to block out the noise.

"Violent crimes—homicides, for instance—I bet it's ten, fifteen times worse on the reservation than it is anywhere else around here.

"The Rainbow Market here is the number-one retail outlet for beer in the state of Oregon. There's a terrible problem down there by the Rainbow boat ramp because the Indians gather down there after they buy beer to drink and panhandle the boaters. There's not much anybody can do about it. If somebody gets a ticket for trespassing, he just laughs it off. What they call 'white man's law' isn't respected by too many people on the reservation.

"One individual over there had a traffic accident, and his wife was turned into a vegetable. She was thrown out of the car and landed face down on the asphalt. It just ground her face off. There was a lot of brain damage. She was only twenty-two. She's still alive, but that's about all. She's in some home, being cared for. The man did some time for it—it was handled federally—and when he got back out, one of the conditions was that he attend treatment. A few days after he finished treatment, he drove drunk up by Simnasho, and when he got stopped, he had some kind of coin that they'd given him at the end of his treatment. This coin had some saying on it that they use, and he seemed to think that the coin meant he wasn't really drunk. That's what he told the policeman who stopped him. I heard about it not long after it happened. But he was so drunk he couldn't stand. And I heard this was a fine guy when he was sober—kind, intelligent. Lots of Indians have signs on their doors, 'No Alcohol or Alcoholics Allowed Inside.' They really try, really struggle with it. Drugs are a tremendous problem now too.

"The law, as a result of what defense attorneys have been doing for years, makes it so difficult to deal with drug problems; it's almost impossible. The police might know somebody's a drug dealer, but that doesn't do any good. The police have to be able to make controlled buys off these people; they have to have reasonable informants—it's incredibly difficult to jump through all the legal hoops in order to arrest and prosecute these people. It's almost as though they have a license to do business and the law allows them to do it. It's a lot more difficult on the reservation than it is anywhere else.

"It takes a lot of time and a lot of money to make an arrest and get a conviction. To do a controlled buy, they have to have a person they're sure will buy the drugs from someone who knows and trusts them. So they usually have to make a deal with somebody who's already been arrested. They have to have a reliable informant. Then, to do the buy, there'd have to be two policemen there to strip-search the informant before he went to make the buy. They have to be absolutely sure the informant doesn't have any drugs of any kind on him. Then they'd give the informant money they'd recorded the serial numbers of to make the buy with. Then they have to keep the informant in constant view until he gets where he's going, and they have to see him clear up until the time he walks into the house. They'd have to hide in the bushes someplace with binoculars. The informant would probably be wired with a recording device, so the police would know what was going on inside. Then they'd see the informant come out, and they'd have to keep him in constant view again until he got to a private place, where they could strip-search him again and take whatever drugs he'd bought as evidence.

"It all sounds pretty difficult, and it's even worse than it sounds. They have to do three of those arrests before they have enough probable cause to fill out an affidavit and ask a judge for a search warrant. Then, once they get the search warrant, will there still be anything there? People who sell drugs move their stuff around all the time. Will they find anything when they finally do get there? If they could use reasonable evidence and go on in and arrest these people and confiscate the drugs and prosecute those people, then they could accomplish something. And it's hardest of all on the reservation, because you have the two systems to go through, and the reservation system doesn't even like having white cops around.

"The young people on the reservation are at least as out of control, as unwilling to listen to adults, to accept authority, as they are in the white world. One of the areas that it's really obvious is that the younger generation has pretty much drifted away from the old culture entirely. The language is dying, other beliefs. It's sad, extremely sad. I have tremendous respect for an Indian person who lives the lifestyle he should and who believes in the Indian culture. I admire them; I really do."

An ancient Ford pulls into a parking place near the Rainbow Market doorway. Two young Indians climb out, one with a large American flag on the front of his T-shirt, the other with bold lettering on the back of his: "Team Ropers Can Handle Anything Horny."

A clean white van parks next to the Ford. The woman in the passenger seat has to be ninety, maybe a hundred years old. She wears a faded blue bandana over snow-white hair, and the gradations of her face are lost in the creases and wrinkles of age. The driver, a middle-aged woman, perhaps a granddaughter, walks into the market and soon emerges with a birthday balloon on a stick. The two young men come out behind her with cans of Coca-Cola.

"It's so unfair to the good people on the reservation that they've made the reservation into a haven for criminals. A tribal member can come over here and commit a crime, a felony crime, and run back on the reservation, and whites can't arrest him over there. In order for white policemen to arrest him, they'd have to get a warrant and take a copy of the warrant down to the tribe, and they have to submit it to the tribal court for them to study, and if the tribal court decides they want to authorize service of that—and they might or they might not—then they send it over to the tribal police department, and it's up to them to make the arrest. So they make the decision: do they want to arrest the guy or not? In the event that they do, and all these hoops have been jumped through, and eventually they do arrest him, then they give the white police a short time, a matter of hours, to get over there and get the guy and get him back over here. Unless it's a major thing, they won't even think about doing it. So what they've done is, they've made the reservation itself a haven for criminals. They cross that bridge, and it's a 'home free' kind of deal.

"They won't allow anything they call 'white man's law' to be used, no matter how reasonable it is. If it's white man's law, they don't want anything to do with it, period. I've heard plenty of Indians say that, repeatedly. It even extends to drunken driving. Over here, if somebody's license is taken away and he drives a car, he gets in trouble, maybe even goes to jail. It's an attempt to keep him from killing the rest of us. They do not recognize any of that on the reservation. They can have a person over there that's been guilty more than once of vehicular homicide, with a dozen convictions for operating under the influence, that's the worst imaginable driver, and it doesn't count. They have the same computer system we have. They put this subject's name in the computer, and — bingo — it comes back and tells you; they can see his whole record, that he's been convicted of vehicular homicide, but it doesn't count.

"Some of these people know that if they come over here they'll get in trouble, so they don't come. They drive drunk on the reservation, but they don't have a serious driving record off the reservation, and as a result of that, because all of that is confidential information within the tribe, insurance companies take a beating. But that's not the worst of it. The worst part is, people are dying.

"One guy'd been in prison for vehicular homicide, and he'd been arrested plenty of times for drunk driving, so he didn't drive off the reservation for a number of years. But he drove on the reservation all the time. One day he had a fight with his girlfriend. They had a baby. One day when they were in the middle of a long fight, he came by his girlfriend's house to pick her up and go driving. They were going to figure out their problems. He was drinking, and they went out toward Dry Creek, and he had an accident right there near the Dry Creek turnoff. He killed her. The baby wasn't breathing when the police arrived, but they brought it back to life — a minor miracle — but the mother died. The reason that happened was, the tribe allowed him to drive on the reservation. If they'd been responsible, that wouldn't have happened. They just don't want anything to do with a white man's law."

Not far down the road from the Rainbow Market, directly opposite the Warm Springs Museum, is the Warm Springs Plaza: Sidaikba Native Collectables, where the merchandise includes T-shirts, blankets, pottery, and arrowheads; the Indian Trail Restaurant, featuring, according to the bright neon in its front windows, espresso and Indian fry bread; Thunderhawk Arts and Crafts, which is supposed to be open, according to the times listed on the front door, but is closed nonetheless; and the Braids'n'Boots Hair Salon, where prices range as follows: Cowboys, $10; Cowgirls, $13; Buckeroos, $7; and Ol' Timers, $5.

An old motor home with a faulty muffler turns into the parking lot, its name — Cherokee Chief — emblazoned in six-inch letters on the side. Just after the motor home has turned off the highway, two police cars and an ambulance speed by, lights flashing and sirens wailing. It turns out that a quarter-mile up the road, in front of the Warm Springs Forest Products Mill, a flat-bed truck has skidded into a ditch and squarely hit a tree.

On an outdoor bench in front of the Braids'n'Boots Hair Salon, a fisherman who has come to the Deschutes for the end of the stone fly hatch talks about the Indians and the river. He is willing to take the time to talk because water released from Pelton Dam has raised the river level and temporarily ruined the dry fly fishing. "I wouldn't miss the stone fly hatch. I've been coming here for the trout more years than I can even remember. Now, the Indians — as far as they're concerned, there's only one fish, a king salmon, a Chinook. Everything else — trout, steelhead, even other kinds of salmon — is a kind of trash fish to them. The tribe closes Sherars Falls when the Chinook runs are really down; I give them credit for that. But they allow terrible abuses in the Zone 6 fishery on the Columbia River.

"Every year the tribes get a week to catch a certain number of fish for cultural and ceremonial purposes. They get a week to catch this certain number, and when they've caught that number, they're supposed to quit. Whether it's the first day or the last day, they're supposed to quit fishing, and if they haven't reached the quota by the last day, they quit anyway.

"Well, for a long time they weren't coming up with the quotas,

TOP *The Warm Springs Plaza*
ABOVE *The Warm Springs Museum* (AUTHOR PHOTOS)

because a lot of fish were being bootlegged. Indians were taking fish out of the nets late at night and not reporting them. Then, in the morning, there'd be a few new fish in the gill nets, and they'd report those. Everybody who knows about fishing around here knows they were doing that. They sold the fish they took out in the night, and they thought they had a right to do that. The Inter-Tribal Fish Commission people know what's going on, but they never try to do much about it.

"There was a guy a while back by the name of Bruce something-

or-other, from Warm Springs, who was captured in a sting opera-tion called Salmon Scam that involved the U.S. Fish and Wildlife Service and some guys from the Natural Resources Department of the tribe, the state police of Oregon and Washington, a whole bunch of people working together. This Bruce and his pals were selling tons of illegal salmon, and the end result of this was that Bruce got sentenced to thirty years in prison. He'd been swindling his own tribe.

"Then a senator from Hawaii named Daniel Inouye interceded and got him out of jail and made it look like he was just a poor oppressed Native American who was trying to make a living. Some-body approached the senator, and, probably because he was a mi-nority senator, he pulled the necessary strings. [Inouye was Japa-nese.] He got the guy released. That was a terrible miscarriage of justice.

"Then Bruce, after he got back, went around telling people the Creator put the salmon there for the Indian people. He said he believed salmon would always be here for Indian people. He even said if he was in a tributary of the river around here somewhere and the only two fish left in that whole system were on a spawn-ing bed, and he needed some salmon, he'd kill them because the Creator would provide more. I guess he must really believe that.

"The Indians think they're right, and they feel like we've in-truded. They believe all of the problems that are happening are our fault. Probably most of them are. The dams and all of the other things that have created the situation we're in now, the Indians are absolutely right. But the reality is, we've got what we've got; the dams are there; the problems are there—so we can't just stand around and throw rocks at each other. We need ways to protect the resource for everybody.

"Ninety percent of the fish are gone because of things that the Indians had nothing to do with. But that's as far as the Indians want to look. Not all of them, but too many of them. Some of them help, but more of them need to.

"Their culture revolves around the Chinook salmon. But we can't have the abuses. After that guy Bruce was convicted, he should have been ostracized from the whole tribe, but what they did was give him a license to go down there to the river and fish again."

 Warm Springs Millennium

A white family—a father and mother with a teenage daughter and younger son between them—walk quickly across the lot from the Indian Trail Restaurant and climb into the "Cherokee Chief." On the third try, the motor starts with a loud, vibrating roar, and they pull out of the lot and turn down the road toward Highway 97.

James Hall

Dr. James Hall graduated from Harvard Medical School, taught at Stanford Medical School, and practiced internal medicine in Medford, Oregon, for twenty years before retiring in 1994 to concentrate on hunting, fishing, and writing.

My understanding of alcoholism is based primarily on the fact that I'm an alcoholic. I'm personally convinced of the scientific data that show a strong genetic predisposition to alcoholism. Both my grandfathers, who were very successful men in their time, died in their early sixties of alcoholic liver disease. Studies show that in an alcoholic, the liver enzymes metabolize in a somewhat different manner. As I recall, alcohol isn't detoxified as fast in the liver, so it gets to the brain sooner and in a more potent form. There are studies of twins who have been separated not long after birth and raised in separate, very different households, and the separations didn't have much effect on the level of alcoholism among these individuals.

Genetic studies throughout the world show very prominent tendencies to alcoholism, or not to alcoholism, depending on the society and the people. For example, peoples who seem very prone to alcoholism are the Irish, areas of Scandinavia, Finland, Russia—and very, very prominently among such peoples are North American Indians. I'm addressing myself to what seem to be genetic matters now, though there are certainly social aspects too.

Research has indicated that most or all American Indians are genetically inclined to alcoholism if they begin to use alcohol. Their chances of abuse and addiction to alcohol are extraordinarily high, some would say as high as 100 percent. I think this is probably the

James Hall (AUTHOR PHOTO)

first and most important thing to understand: alcoholism is an inherited disease.

Of course, with sufficient and adequate education, becoming an alcoholic can be avoided no matter what your genetic predisposition is; and if you do become one, of course you can get into recovery, as I have. You can do whatever it takes. But it definitely isn't easy.

I believe that if one has become an alcoholic — and there are various definitions of that, but it seems to me you're an alcoholic if drinking interferes in an uncontrollable way with many, if not all, aspects of your life: relationships and job might be the two most obvious and important factors.

But some alcoholics can function on their jobs despite the drinking. Have you ever heard of alcoholic blackouts? I'll tell you one story. This is true, told to me by an airline pilot. He reported to work once after a long bout of drinking. He'd cleaned himself, showered, used mouthwash and all that, so nobody could even tell he'd been drinking. Well, on the way to the airport he just blacked out. In other words, afterwards he had no recollection of anything he did. When he snapped out of it, he was in his plane, speeding along a runway. But he didn't even know if he was taking off or landing. For two or three seconds he was terrified, because he had no idea what to do. Then he looked at the fuel gauges, and the tanks were full, so he knew he was taking off, and he went ahead and finished the job. Physicians have done delicate surgery — perfectly successful surgery — while completely blacked out.

The only successful way to get into recovery is through abstinence, and that usually needs to go along with changing the habits of life, some kind of program for living which displaces some of the time and energy spent with alcohol. I've adopted the Alcoholics Anonymous program, which has been widely successful in many countries of the world.

I'm very fond of alcohol; that's the curse. I'm fond of alcohol, and I don't want to ever take another drink. It's an old and often repeated story: alcoholics who think they're cured try to drink socially, and they're soon ruined again. There's kind of a joke in AA: if you think you can drink like a gentleman, go ahead and do it. But hardly anybody — maybe nobody — can actually do it. I'm dedicated to working on changing my life, improving my spirituality; that's the vital issue as far as I'm concerned. The twelve steps of AA are adopted from the world's oldest religions. Much of it relates in a direct way to the Ten Commandments.

In a way, of course, it's very simple: just don't drink. But you also have to change your whole life, which isn't so simple. It's not a matter of willpower; it's almost the opposite. Total surrender is what seems to work. Surrender seems to bring strength.

I've emphasized genetic factors, which certainly applies to me, and to most others, but there's no question that social factors also play a very important part. So if you have the genetics and something goes wrong socially, it's a terrible double whammy.

In my case there are excuses. There almost always are. My job as a physician was extraordinarily stressful, so I thought I needed some kind of escape, something to get my mind off my responsibilities for a while. Most of us have tragedies in our lives, and mine included the sudden death of my daughter in a skiing accident. I'd not been drinking for a while before that happened.

But I think if you're really an alcoholic, you can take a drink because you're sad or stressed, or you can drink to celebrate. There's usually an excuse to drink if you want to give in to it.

The amount that one drinks isn't always related to being an alcoholic. There are so-called social drinkers who often drink very heavily, and they may not be alcoholics, because alcohol doesn't take over their lives. There are alcoholics who may drink only occasionally, but things like this will happen—and I've heard variations of this story many times: A person may be abstinent for a long time, never even thinking about drinking. He's going to an important business meeting somewhere in another city, and he'll wake up three weeks later in Manila, having no idea how he got there or what he's been doing, after having taken one cocktail on the plane. That's another of those total blackouts.

My heart goes out to alcoholics. I've been around so many of them, and I'm involved with local treatment programs. I've found that many—maybe most—people with alcoholism are intelligent, sensitive, decent. Maybe I'm prejudiced, but sometimes they seem, as a group, potentially more capable than the general population. There are wonderful people, charming people, in spite of this terrible disease they have.

I'm afraid alcoholics often tend to lie to themselves—like the Indian who showed his medal when a policeman stopped him for driving drunk. That's what we call classic denial. Denial can be so profound. I've talked to alcoholics dying from the extremes of the disease, and they swear until the end that alcohol isn't what's killing them. They truly believe that, or they want to believe it. I've talked to people who drove the wrong way down the freeway drunk, and they deny that alcohol had anything to do with it.

We speak of recovering rather than recovery. I've been sober and happy for a long period of time, but still consider myself recovering and think I'm at risk forever. I have no desire to drink—don't even think about it—and I'm happy; nevertheless, I never completely relax.

Most people, including myself, get into recovery programs because of a crisis. We hit a personal bottom. We go so low we give up. That bottom can be very low—lying in the gutter, or in jail. Suicide is very common among alcoholics. In my own case, I hit my bottom for the last time, I think, when I'd already gone through divorce and a good many losses, including very prominently my daughter. I still had a very good job, was respected and had a nice home, and lived well, but I knew it was the bottom. I wanted to recover.

One of the most profound things that happens is, if you're around people in recovery, they're so glad they're getting better. You see that, and it makes you almost frightened, and you say, "I want some of that." That was my experience.

I think people who work in recovery, counselors and such, should be alcoholics themselves. You can't really understand unless you've been through the experience yourself. In my opinion, that's far more important than any academic credentials. Doctors, as a group, are poorly trained and rather stupid about alcoholism. But an addict that may never have gotten out of high school, or grade school for that matter, can be profoundly helpful working with another addict.

If a person is trying hard to get into recovery, but his life doesn't get better—all the external circumstances of his life—if he doesn't start feeling that things are improving, then why not drink? If the social conditions don't improve, recovery is a lot more difficult. Of course, the individual can help make conditions improve himself, but he can't do everything.

I have some strong feelings about the way our society deals with alcoholism and drug addiction, and the way our politicians abuse the issue. We really should legalize certain drugs. An alcoholic will always find alcohol, and any desperate addict will find what he wants, no matter how far he has to go or what he has to do. I know that liquor is illegal on Indian reservations. Prohibition proved that making a substance illegal doesn't work. An alcoholic will drink after-shave lotion, methyl alcohol from antifreeze, which blinds you. An uneducated, untreated alcoholic will end up dead by suicide or an accident, or insane. That may come later in life, but it also might come to someone quite young. Drugs and alcohol decimate people's lives, always. I know a man who had a shotgun in his mouth, and the gun misfired when he pulled the trigger with his toe. He got into recovery just after that, and today he seems to be fine.

Education and treatment are the only hope. And the social factors. People have to have the opportunities for decent work, decent lives, afterwards. The people that work in the field know how wrong the politicians are. This year the state of Oregon is supposedly spending more on prisons than on education. It's so sad to me, this "three strikes and you're out" thing going on now. People with an inherited disease are sentenced to years, decades in jail, when what they need is treatment. What they're in jail for isn't really a moral failure at all. When the head of a household is put in a prison, there's a widening circle that affects many other people in his family, his whole circle of acquaintances. The financial loss to our whole society is just enormous. I just don't think addiction is a moral offense. What we do now is like jailing diabetics.

You asked me about recovery rates. Among physicians, the recovery rate is quite high, and I think that's because we have so much to lose. If, let's say, you're a poor Indian on a reservation, or a poor black in the middle of East LA, what do you have to lose? Maybe you've already lost your wife; you've lost your car; you don't have a job anyway. So what do you have to lose? I stood to lose my medical license, something extraordinarily valuable to me, something that I worked twelve years to get.

The politicians are like the uninformed doctors who just do not understand the disease process. I also think our policies are influenced by moralists, but this isn't a moral issue. Maybe our politicians are living in terror of those fundamentalists. Anyway, if I'd been on a reservation, or someplace in the inner city, I might not have made it. To make it, you've definitely got to have some hope.

James Hall

Sue Terran

In 1972 Sue Terran helped found the Siskiyou Health Clinic in Josephine County. In those days, the primary purpose of the clinic was to serve the area's large "hippie" population. Today, with Sue's partnership, it has become the primary health care provider for tens of thousands of rural Oregonians. As part of a program at the University of Washington focused on training rural primary-care Physician Assistants (she was the top student in her class), she lived for half a year on the Warm Springs Reservation and worked in the clinic there.

Sue Terran (AUTHOR PHOTO)

There's some racial tension at Warm Springs. A lot of the things teenagers do are racially motivated. There are ongoing struggles going on between the natives, the Hispanics, and the whites. However, on the reservation you see an amazing number of intermarriages between those three groups. And in Madras you see it. It may be what needs to happen, because, speaking from a totally medical viewpoint, you take three tribes of people and put them all together since 1855—so that's, what, five generations, maybe— by the time you've done that, everybody's marrying everybody's third or fourth cousin, so there are a lot of genetic problems.

Nearly everybody knows about the alcoholism and diabetic problems in native populations. But there are these other conditions that I didn't know about until I got there. The occurrence is really high for rheumatoid arthritis, lupus, and sclera derma— these and other auto-immune disorders. It's probably precipitated by all those generations of intermarriage. These are all terribly debilitating diseases, so it's a serious problem. It's hard for physically disabled people to live in rural areas, just plain physically hard. There aren't any wheelchair ramps; it's difficult for them just to get in and out of cars.

Up until about two and a half years ago, the old clinic at Warm Springs wasn't much bigger than this room [we are eating dinner at a small Mexican restaurant], and it served the entire reservation. The tribe was informed that they were number twenty-eight or something on the government waiting list for a new facility. Maybe they'd get it in the year 2010 or something. What they did was build—I think I remember this accurately—a fourteen-million-dollar facility. The tribe held meetings and decided to build it themselves.

The agreement that the government made in 1855 was to provide medical care to the reservation. In 1855, what did that mean? A guy on his horse with his old medical bag and maybe his Bible. They had no idea about cat scans or antibiotics. But it's a government agreement, so the tribe built its own facility, and the government staffs it. All the staff are federal employees.

This clinic has six dentists, including a pediatric dentist, an oral surgeon, the highest-tech equipment you can imagine. They have a lab that's better than most labs around here: their own X-ray equipment, their own ultrasound. They employed native furniture makers and weavers, so the design and furnishings are a work of art. Every chair is covered with a tapestry. The drapes are hand woven.

Sue Terran

It's all just gorgeous, true native handiwork. And along with it, they have state-of-the-art computer technology.

The tribe also decided to establish their own health management organization. They take the federal funds they get for each native person on the reservation and pool it all together. If I saw a patient that needed to be referred to a specialist, there were certain standards that were okay, no problem, and there were other standards that had to go to the committee to be decided.

That committee made decisions based on a lot of cultural perspectives. For instance: "Look, we've spent fifty thousand dollars over the last ten years sending this guy to drug and alcohol rehab and in-patient treatment, and we even sent him to Seattle, and he's still drinking. That's enough." There was lots of compassion, and they gave people lots of breaks, but they also had a sense, you know, "Let's invest this money into this child instead."

There was a guy who had a terrible knife wound across his cheek and wanted plastic surgery to repair it. Well, he started the fight, so it's his problem, and he deserves to keep the scar. These decisions were based on moral judgements about whether the health problem was self-inflicted or not. How much compassion could they have for somebody who'd done it to himself?

There's definitely conflict between modern medicine and tradition on the reservation. For one thing, there's this whole ethic of stoicism. And there's a tradition of not making eye contact. I'd been taught that you always make eye contact, to engage the person to be open with you and tell you what's wrong, what's going on. Well, you interview somebody there, and often you get these one- or two-word answers from people who stare down at the floor:

"Why are you here?"

"Because."

Or, "How long have you had this pain?"

"A while."

Getting detail is really hard—less so with the younger people, because they're more outgoing. But a lot of people forty and over still have that stoicism.

I remember one man: I did an exam on him, and he was acting kind of shy. It turned out he didn't want me to see his appendectomy scar. As soon as I saw it, I said, "Oh, you've had your appendix out." He was so ashamed. He said, "If only I'd stayed in the sweat lodge longer. If only I'd taken all those herbs that grandma gave me. If only I'd prayed harder. I could have cured myself." But his appendix ruptured, and he nearly died. Finally, his relatives drove him off to the hospital. I said, "Aren't you grateful that they saved your life?" And he answered, "No, I should have died rather than live with this shame."

Another guy came into the clinic limping a little bit. "What happened?" I asked him. "Well, I fell and hit my leg on a rock." I asked him, "Are you in a lot of pain?" and he just shrugged. I should've realized that's the one thing you never ask. To admit pain is a kind of disgrace. You can't judge native people by white standards. This guy had his thigh bone sticking out of his leg underneath his Levi's. He just didn't want to tell me anything. He knew something was terribly wrong, but he didn't want to admit it.

You can't tell anything by facial expressions. Little kids are taught not to show pain. You don't cry when you get a shot, or when you're getting sutured. Family members tell the children, "Come on, don't cry. Be brave."

Who you should really interview are two doctors who work at the clinic and live beside Warm Springs. They've both been there — I forget if it's twenty or twenty-five years. They're just amazing men. I loved working with them. They're part of the community. They're both whites, but they're part of the tribe. They've even decided to raise their own kids along with the natives. When I was there they gave a party for the doctors, and the elders came, and the chiefs came, and at the clinic they provided a sit-down barbecue dinner for hundreds and hundreds of people. They love feasts. Feasting is truly a part of the culture.

Because it's so close to the Oregon Health Sciences University in Portland, which has a large training hospital and medical school, the reservation is on a normal route for medical students and dental students. There's a regular stream that go there for their rotation, but usually it's just for a week or a month. Mine was very rare, because it was six months. So I was there long enough to help rather than hinder, which is what student training sometimes does. It was very satisfying; I loved it, and when it was time to go, I was sad.

What I loved was the sense of community, a sense of belonging. I don't want to totally romanticize that, but it's something that I appreciate here where I live too. It's really lost in American culture. People move so much, especially out west here. People are removed from their roots so much that it's pretty rare to find some who have been in any one spot for twenty years, let alone several generations. And even though it's not really their native land at Warm Springs, it's their roots, and they've made it that way. The people are tied into each other. For instance, there's a problem with alcoholism, but it's not like you see in the white community, where people would be lying in the gutters suffering from malnutrition and disease, because everyone is somebody's relative. If you've got a problem, you have family around you all the time. It's not always harmonious, but it's real.

You see every part of the spectrum on the reservation. You see absolute traditionalists who live very austere lives and follow the red path and honor their ancestors. Then you see people who seem to dress and live just like white people do, but who really respect many aspects of their culture and religion and retain a lot of it in their lives. You see others who are very cynical and having a hard time. You see separate, depressed, very extreme poverty families that are really in trouble, really in crisis.

They were very relieved when I was there—the native people I connected with—to hear my stories about living in a predominantly white community. They were relieved when I told them that the problems they're having are the problems I see right here in Cave Junction. These problems are related to poverty and ignorance and losing touch with their roots.

My personal belief is that the greatest harm that ever happened to native people was the government putting their children in the live-in dormitory schools. It totally destroyed two generations of families, and they'll never really recover. These people now are adults trying to raise children, and they don't have a clue what a family's all about, so they have to rely on the elders. It's like a whole generation missed everything—not just what it's like to be a native person, but what it's like to be in any kind of family unit. They were totally separated from their parents. They were even forbidden to write letters to their families. They were forbidden to have a picture of their parents in their dorm rooms. I saw the extent of what that did.

I think the life expectancy for a native male is forty-four and for a female is fifty-four. That makes the life expectancy for native people worse than most third-world countries. Mostly it's attributable to trauma, and to drug- and alcohol-related problems. I was just astounded when I was there about how many die. There's deaths and funerals all the time.

It's a sweeping generalization, but tribal members would agree with this: risk-taking is really at the root of a lot the deaths—physical risk-taking, something as simple as car seats for babies. Of course, they use cradle boards, but even convincing people to strap the cradle boards in the car or use any kind of restraint is difficult. That feeling of prevention—teaching your two-year-old not to touch the hot stove—that's not always done. It's like they have to just let kids do what they do, learn lessons for themselves. But that's not a traditional belief; in my mind, it's what happened to two generations who never learned how to parent, how to be assertive with a child and realize that a child needs guidance and compassion.

Certainly in ancient times children were surrounded by the tight-knit group of the tribe and the community and had the input and instruction of lots of people. Doing health care with children at Warm Springs was really, really challenging. So there you are, at work in a clinic, and here's this five-year-old with a fever, and the kid is brought in by auntie and grandma. So you say, "Well, how long has he had the fever?" "Well, I don't know. Last night he was with grandma, and the night before he was with so-and-so auntie, and the night before that he stayed with so-and-so." Nobody really knows what this kid's been up to. I ask, "Has he thrown up, has he done this or that?" Nobody knows. And that's because kids belong to the group. They benefit from that, but there's also a lack of continuity regarding all the stuff that kids go through. There's little continuity, stability, or predictability. Having a bedroom where their own toys are—that's just not in the concept.

I didn't notice much tension between the different tribes at Warm Springs. There are so many mixed groups and families at this point. They all share an amazing child development center, with over three hundred kids there, from birth to age four. They have special programs for disabled kids. Their kids get the best. There's a real understanding that they'll lose their way of life if they don't do something totally different with the new generation.

But the problems start when they go to school in Madras. I took care of lots of high-school kids who got in fights at school—fist fights, knife fights, rock fights. Here I am, a student learning how to suture, trying to do the perfect suture job. I'm putting in this extreme care not to leave a scar. That's my training. Then when these boys come in for their follow-ups, they've taken the dressings off, taken their own stitches out. "Why do you do that?" I ask them. They *want* the scar. They're very proud of their scars. It's a battle scar, even when you're six years old and you cut your knee falling off your bicycle. It means you've suffered, and you've survived.

I lived right in the town of Warm Springs, in one of those white government houses near the clinic. I walked to work. Sometimes when they had ceremonies, the drums would go on all night long. There's a huge gathering the third week in June, Pi-Ume-Sha, Treaty Days, an international gathering, and it's just great. They come weeks ahead of time with campers and trailers and tipis. When I was there, they had their parades and dancing when it was 108 degrees. They didn't stop or even slow down. Their endurance is amazing.

I've done lots of sweat lodges. When you're in there, you really think you're going to die. They like that feeling—pushing yourself to the absolute maximum of your endurance, and surviving.

The Warm Springs people were so gracious to me, the most welcoming, hospitable people I've known. I was treated wonderfully. People invited me over to dinner, to family gatherings, to sweat lodges, funerals, births, to longhouse gatherings with storytelling.

They have lots and lots of meetings at Warm Springs. At their meetings everyone has a chance to—and is expected to—participate. It doesn't matter if things go on for eight hours. When they want to, the people become very verbal and eloquent, and they just go on and on, which is a great thing—part of the social connection.

Living all these years in Takilma, I've tried to imagine what it would be like if our community was completely separate from the state of Oregon and the United States. What if we were our own little nation here? What if we had to run our own power company, build our own roads? We already have our own school and clinic, our own work co-op. But what if we really had to do everything? That's what they do at Warm Springs. They have countless meetings lasting hours talking about trash pick-up, about upgrading electrical systems, about the water supply.

An interesting thing that happened while I was there was a decision they made that way. You know the layout of the land, mostly lava and barren desert. But they have some small woodland areas, and they were logging them. An environmental expert said to them, "Look, three or four more years, and this will be gone." So most of the logging came to a screeching halt, and suddenly, one of their biggest employers was gone.

They'd been fighting the idea of a casino for years and years. Then they had some community meetings, hundreds of people arguing for hours and hours. There were a lot of reasons not to want to put a casino in, but the reality is, this casino's for Portland rich people. That resort is for rich people. But it's a way for the tribe to support itself. The casino is really a way to replace the logging industry.

They also took the mill and converted it, to use what wood they still had to build furniture rather than produce lumber from logs. That way, they can cut fewer trees and employ more people to make hand-crafted articles. There are some very smart and future-thinking, creative people on the reservation.

The tribal justice system can be harsh. Most of the tribal police are whites. One of the meetings I went to when I was there was between the elders and the tribal police department. They wanted to make peace, and that went on for hours and hours. It was very touching and really very wonderful. This was the situation: When you enter the longhouse, there's a sacred way to do it. You face a certain direction, and after you enter the doorway, you turn in a certain direction. You greet whoever is there, and you don't interrupt whatever happens to be going on.

Well, there was a guy who was wanted for a crime, and the tribal police burst in on a ceremony to look for this suspect. They very rudely dishonored all of the traditions. They could easily have waited two hours or whatever it took to see whether this guy was even there or not. He wasn't going to sneak out. But the tribal police weren't native, so they weren't honoring tribal tradition. Everyone at the meeting wanted crime to be dealt with, but in a way that wasn't rude and disruptive. And by the end of the meeting, they worked it out.

Something I shared with people I encountered there was something that hadn't occurred to many of them. I told them how envious I was that they knew their roots. Here I am, a mongrel breed of probably eight or ten different origins from all over the world. I told them how I grew up, always wanting to be *something*. When I was a little kid I used to lie to the kids at school and tell them I was born in Ireland, just so I could feel like I was from *somewhere*. But at Warm Springs their roots are real.

I had a two-story, five-bedroom house mostly to myself for six months. Once in a while, a short-term student who just needed a place to stay would come by. Lots of different students came in and out for a week or two. Some of them were so horrified, so frightened, that they'd commute a hundred miles one-way back and forth to Portland instead of staying overnight on the reservation. That's just absolute racism, ignorance. I felt just the opposite. I wanted to be there all the time.

The museum put on a wonderful play while I was there. It was written by tribal members who started their own little performance group. One of the scenes of this play involved a fourteen- or fifteen-year-old boy who was just completely punked out — a gang member with all those clothes and metal spikes. His grandpa was a chief with full feather headgear. There was a long dialogue with the two of them trying to honor and accept each other, as grandfather and grandson, yet realizing they were from such different worlds. Several scenes were on the same theme: How do we keep our traditions? How do we live in the modern world? How do we let our kids watch TV all day and expect them to honor the old ways? They know the dilemma. They're very well aware of it. And in the spirit of endurance, they don't give up on trying to make it work.

Wilson Wewa Jr.

Wilson Wewa Jr., a Northern Paiute, served for several years as director of the Culture and Heritage Office at the Warm Springs Reservation, an office housed in a red brick building near the elementary school in the town of Warm Springs. In the reception area is a conspicuous sign that reads: *They are young once but Indian forever.*

On 10 August 1997, the Portland *Oregonian* reported that two twelve-year-old Warm Springs boys had squirmed through a small window in a double-wide trailer that serves as part of the reservation's Culture and Heritage compound. The young vandals smashed computers, poured sugar into VCRs, and destroyed disks that contained recorded legends told by elders long deceased, as well as many transcriptions of the Wasco, Paiute, and Sahaptin languages. Identified from a videotape taken during a break-in at a nearby market, the boys were arrested the following day. Our interview with Wilson Wewa Jr. began with this sad subject.

Our office has tried to recoup everything that was lost in that vandalism incident. People responded really quickly in helping us to try to salvage some of our work. When the kids broke in, they broke up a whole bunch of computer monitors, destroyed one of our hard drives on the computer, and then they got into our floppies and literally busted all the casings open and exposed the recorder instruments inside. And we had, I think it was about twenty-five disks that were broken open.

We talked to our computer people upstairs in this building, the ones who teach computer classes and stuff, to see what kind of knowledge they had. They told us they could try using water, so they washed everything they could and hung it all up to air

Wilson Wewa Jr. (AUTHOR PHOTO)

dry. Then they put everything in separate computer sleeves so they wouldn't get magnetized or whatever it is that happens. They made insurances that no more damage than had already happened would occur.

Then as people read the stories in the *Oregonian*, we had folks that just called to express their concern, their outrage over what had happened to all of the work that we're trying to do for the tribes in maintaining and preserving the languages and culture for our future. Regular people called from wherever the media touched, and we even got a call from Microsoft up in Seattle.

Wilson Wewa Jr.

But I guess the quickest response was from the couple from Vancouver, Washington, that run a computer store, a private business, independent of the brand-name places. They told us that so many of the things that they hear about on the TV from around the world, the starvation, the wars, Sarejevo, the Middle East, all of the things happening, that all of us, including them as individuals, have no control over. So they decided that this was something that fell within their control, a problem they could do something about, and they drove down with a whole carload of equipment—computer monitors and keyboards, casings, and things like that—and they set it all up back in our language trailer.

They took our damaged goods and started retrieving information, using two or three different programs. If they didn't get it with one program, then they tried another one. They were able to keep pulling off more and more. At the end of two days, they'd probably recovered 90 percent of our material. For the material that wasn't recoverable, they had more technology that wasn't able to be transported down here, so they took what they needed of ours back to Vancouver and worked on it at their office during their spare time.

I think when they were done, we recovered probably about 98 percent, if not 100 percent, of everything that was lost. We might have got it all, because we got an impression that on one of the disks, or even more than one, there were programs that whoever was working on them entered in titles but actually never entered anything more, so there was really nothing there to retrieve. The evidence leads us to believe that there's a good possibility we recovered 100 percent.

Do you think the boys that broke in and did the damage actually knew what they were doing?

It wasn't only boys. It was boys and girls. On our reservation we're having to start to deal with gangs. It's real sad, but the ones that broke in were our own thirteen- to fifteen-year-olds. Pretty young. And what the intent of them breaking in to our trailer was—I don't know.

I don't think their intent was to destroy something of the magnitude of what they destroyed, as much as it was just to destroy *something.* My speculation is that they got in there, and somebody broke something, and so somebody else had to top it. And in the process, it escalated until they just trashed the place, almost like a feeding frenzy of sharks or something, piranhas. That's what happened. And after they saw what they did, they probably regretted it, but the damage was done.

We're trying to get through to our children. We started last year, or a year and a half ago, to try to develop a curriculum to implement into our school system. In the past we did have individuals, elders and other people, who went into the school and talked in their native languages, taught the names of animals and other general words, and that was somewhat successful. But it wasn't a formal curriculum, and in today's world everything has to be down on paper and acknowledged by academia. So our old way didn't have the necessary structure.

Now, through various grants and tribal monies, we were able to get a curriculum developer to help us start creating a language program for kids. We knew from the start that we couldn't meet the needs of every age group on our reservation, and we know that the strongest learning processes start in children from the time they're born and last clear up until the time they're about five years old. So the decision was made to introduce language at the youngest level, in kindergarten.

This year we introduced language in kindergarten, which raised a problem, because we haven't had a real good response from the community for meeting the needs for next year. Our teachers are teaching in kindergarten and at the same time developing a language curriculum for next year, for first grade. But we don't have a pool of teachers to allow us to start teaching language in the first grade next year while we keep on teaching it in kindergarten. As the program grows there'll be levels of teaching throughout the system that will follow the kids. When you teach kids to read, you teach them the alphabet first, and then the sounds, the phonetics, and then you start teaching them to read and identify. It's always more and more advanced. We're faced with that problem, with not having enough people.

Wilson Wewa Jr.

We just don't have a pool of teachers. We have a lot of good people in the community that would be good teachers, but none of them have stepped forward to say, "I think that's something worthy of my time, and I want to be a part of it. I want to give the community something back, something to help develop our people."

Along with the language is the culture. It's true that the government boarding schools took away our traditional ways of teaching and destroyed the cohesiveness of families. As a result, we have generations of young people that don't know how to be parents, that don't have the skills of basic survival. They don't have the teachings that make them able to be providers. And I say provider in the more traditional sense of times past, when our people depended each day on whatever their hands were able to make or whatever their bodies were able to procure for their needs, for the basics of food and shelter.

Some of the elder people have brought that kind of teaching forward and given it a little twist. They say that because we no longer rely entirely on hunting, fishing, and gathering roots and berries, we can still maintain our families by educating ourselves and joining the work force or the tribal organization to provide for our families monetarily. Nowadays we have to be able to go to the grocery store and buy our needs. We have to be able to buy a house, to get transportation.

Because the basic survival skills of our people have been taken away, many of them have become dependent on programs like welfare and some of the other social service stuff. It's gotten so bad today that we have babies raising babies. And if those babies don't have the skills to survive, their children will be even worse off. In my eyes, we're in danger of forming a society of people that are far too dependent on somebody else to provide for them.

In the past, our people always used to help one another out. My grandmother told me how, a long time ago, she heard stories from her dad, and from his old people, aunts and uncles. They talked about times of plenty, and also about times of very meager pickings. Those who weren't fortunate enough to be in an area where there was plenty of food to harvest during the harvesting time, or who belonged to a family without a lot of sons and daughters that could gather enough for the winter, anybody who ran out—the other people always shared with them. Our people helped one another survive, even if it meant total starvation for the village.

All people worked in those days. There was no time to be lazy. Laziness meant death a long time ago. Everybody was a provider in some form. Even the little kids had their place within the family, their contributions. When they were old enough, they watched the smallest children while the adults hunted and gathered. Grandma and grandpa made winter clothes or sewed moccasins. People whose bodies weren't strong enough to walk long distances maybe made baskets. Everybody had a place in the society.

But today there are some of our young people that are always in the community with their hands out, with their little cups, standing here and there, saying, "Pardon me. Contribute to my cause." And it's not only weak people. Shamefully, it's some of our young men, able bodied and strong enough to hold a job; but they've learned to become dependent on social programs.

So our people are having a hard time; but I don't think it's only happening to our people, Indian people—it's happening to other groups. Native Americans are still at the low end of the population scale, but I think I've read that today even white people aren't what you call a true majority anymore. It's happening in all the ethnic groups, this dependency on federal programs, state programs, and in the case of Native Americans, on our own tribal programs.

I think the problems have to do with values. A long time ago, our people foraged for food, and today we have to work. We no longer have nuclear families. When I was growing up I lived in a poor place, but I wasn't really poor. If we use white man's standards, then it was poor. We lived in a two-bedroom house, and then my uncle built another room on. Our aunt lived in a one-room house nearby. An uncle had a one-room house nearby. Our grandma and grandpa had another one-room house. We were close together, and we took care of one another. If my parents were gone somewhere, my aunts or uncles kept an eye on us, or our grandma and grandpa did. There was always that cohesiveness. When we went to the rural area where our grandma and grandpa's ranch was, even there our family was at least within a mile of one another, and we always looked out for one another. Older cousins took care of younger cousins. That was a duty.

It's my opinion that when people start getting educated—and I think this happens in all cultures when there's a move from what you might call primitive to civilized—there are some people who are enthralled with wanting to become civilized, and they assimilate real quickly. They become like white people. They put their own values behind, and then they start thinking that because they've assimilated, that's the best thing for the rest of their people to do.

Because of that, decisions are made that hurt those that can't advance as quickly, and we leave a whole bunch of people behind. That's what's happened here. Our reservation has advanced so quickly that we've left a whole lot of people behind. We haven't taught them how to survive.

There have been friends of the tribes for as long as I can remember that were non-Indians, that work in the communities that surround Warm Springs. Then there are those people who could care less what happens here, as long as it doesn't overflow into their community. They don't care, but once it does flow into their community, then they have something to say about it, and a lot of times, they don't know anything about us. They voice their misconceptions about what's happening here on the reservation, and it's ignorance. They don't choose to know; they don't want to know; so they base opinions on ignorance.

One day years ago I was over in the truck stop in Madras. The truck stop is a gathering place for most of the retired non-Indian people—ranchers, old geezers—they gather over there at lunchtime at the truck stop and drink coffee and eat lunch together. I happened to walk in there one day to have lunch, and one guy didn't see me come in, and I sat behind him. He'd just finished reading one of the local so-called newspapers, and he was voicing his opinion about the educational system and the burden that Warm Springs was placing on the school district. He thought it was about time that the federal government quit spending so much money on the

Indians at Warm Springs. His idea was that we were taking their part of the pie.

Well, he had some of his partners sitting there that were facing me, and they were trying to inconspicuously get his attention, to slow him down on what he was saying, but he was on the roll. He talked about how much was spent on educating Indians, all of it to no avail. I was going to let it pass, but his words were so biased and ignorant that I couldn't, and I finally got up from where I was sitting and went over and tapped him on the shoulder.

I told him, "I couldn't help but overhear what you're talking about. I take it you're one of the local farmers from this area. You've probably been here all your life. But I'll have you know that if the tribes didn't sign to have the dams on our eastern river—that's the Deschutes River—there would be no income from those dams for the county. So we provide income for you, because we have the say-so over what those dams produce in irrigation and revenue. You get some cream off of the top of the revenue that those dams bring in."

Then I told him about the block grants that are allocated to school districts for minorities. If you look at it, Warm Springs is getting pretty close to becoming 50 percent of the students in the district. If it wasn't for the Indian kids, there wouldn't be a lot of the block grant monies. I told him, without Warm Springs Reservation being their neighbor and part of the county, they might be hurting. If the tribes ever decided to build a school, grades K through 12, and those block grant monies started coming in directly to the tribe, the school district in Madras would be hurting.

I think the statistics show that Jefferson County has the lowest property tax rate in the state of Oregon, and that's because the county has a lot of programs that are supplemented by the tribes living right next door to the white community. If our tribes ever pulled out, then that old man could bellyache, because then his property taxes would go up. A lot of farmers would end up folding because they wouldn't be able to make ends meet without the Indians' help. I told that guy he'd better do some work and educate himself before he starts sounding off on something he doesn't know anything about.

When I was done, one of his partners across the table told him,

"I always knew one of these days you'd bite off more than you could chew! Sometimes your mouth just goes on and on, and I think you've just been put back in your place today."

That old man sat there, and the tips of his ears turned red, and his face got red, and then I went and sat back down. That was the first time I ever got a feel of the ignorance of somebody who was probably in his sixties or seventies and lived right next door. If he really had been a lifetime resident of Jefferson County, and it's pretty much for sure he was, that really was ignorance about our county and about what happens here on the reservation. And he'd probably had that same viewpoint since he was a young guy. It probably festered through all the years.

One of the biggest debates I have in my mind relates to when I was in school, when the educational system seemed more friendly toward kids. When I was in grade school, the teachers in Warm Springs stayed right here on the reservation. They participated in Warm Springs community events. They were a real identity on the reservation. But now we have mostly teachers that commute from outside. They come here only to teach, and then they go back and live on the outside. We have a high turnover rate of teachers in the elementary school, so in my eyes we don't get the continuity we need. The teachers don't get to know the people they're serving as well as they should. Because of all the changing faces, in my eyes it's as if children enter the educational arena as wards of the court. It's similar to when kids get pulled out of dysfunctional families and sent to foster homes. It's that same way with the kids in school when they don't get that continuity. Kids grow up and never identify with who their teachers are, so it throws another stumbling block in their way when they're trying to find out who they are.

I think it has a lot to do, too, with the growing population of our county. Even Madras doesn't have very many teachers that stay in the county, because we're too rural. A lot of teachers don't want to be in these rural areas; they'd rather be in larger towns. So the turnover is high there too.

The classrooms are so overcrowded that you don't get the bonding between the teachers and students. When I left this reservation in the sixth grade—that would have been 1967—and commuted to junior high in Madras, the school was still small enough so that when Indian kids weren't meeting standards, teachers took the time to help them identify what the problem was and then to overcome that problem.

I had one friend who had a serious learning disability, and as a result of the teachers' helping him, he finally excelled academically in high school and became a varsity football and basketball player for the school, too. It was all because the teachers took the time to help him overcome his problem. He truly excelled. But that kind of thing isn't happening as much anymore.

Another problem that we're starting to have—it's not all a Hispanic problem, but as the borders from Mexico have become more open, we have more migrant families coming in here to Oregon, because Oregon is an agricultural state. It attracts the migrant families, the seasonal workers. Trying to meet that need of seasonal students coming into our communities has thrown another wrench into the works.

When I try to look back and see whether there was any split between the races, between the whites and Indians kids, a long time ago when I was in junior high and high school—I didn't see it that much. We were smaller, and I just didn't see it that much. I knew people were cliquish. Athletes stuck together; academic guys—the nerds or whatever you call them—they hung together. And in a way, it was just like society—there was a lower class, a middle class, and an upper class in the school. But you still had groups of peers that were mixed racially—Indians, whites, Hispanics.

In those days you had Hispanic families that had been in Jefferson County for two or three generations. They got along; they intermixed; they dated. We had some marriages after graduation, Hispanics and whites, Hispanics and Indians. You don't have that now.

The other day I was listening to some people talking about what's happening in the school, and they said they're having fights between the Hispanic kids and the white kids, between the Hispanic kids and the Indian kids. That kind of stuff is getting worse.

Wilson Wewa Jr.

Bunches of kids are ganging up on single people. They bust cars up. It's not safe for anybody's children to be by themselves in town after a certain time of night.

But I didn't hear too much when I was listening to that conversation about conflicts between the Indian kids and the white kids of Madras. Maybe the fact that I was sitting there had an effect on the conversation, but maybe not. It made me start to wonder whether it's because the migrant people move in and then out of places after a short time that's causing so many problems. If you look at it, people that are just passing through a community, in any society or culture, can have an adverse effect on that community. They don't have ownership, so they have nothing to lose. This may be the only month or the only season that they're in your community, so they don't care, because next month, or next year, they'll be someplace else.

I have to remember at the same time, though, that we have kids right here on the reservation that are vandalizing our buildings, spray painting, busting cars, busting street lights—and this is our community.

Are there things that are getting better instead of worse on the reservation? Or that at least show signs that they might improve in the future?

One of my greatest hopes as the director of our cultural office here is to introduce our cultural ways into the school curriculum. Back in the late sixties and early seventies, they had a culture camp here in Warm Springs, where some of the elders participated. It was run out of this office. They taught dances and songs and some of the language in a camp up in the mountains. At that time, I was just a teenager—fourteen, fifteen years old—and that had a big impact on my life.

For years we haven't had a camp like that. We did have a 4-H camp that tried to add a facet of culture, but they didn't have the know-how pertaining to what's important—or if they knew what was important, they didn't know how to implement it.

Something related to this is the fact that I worked for sixteen years in the senior citizen program. I had the confidence of all the seniors during those years, and many of the seniors that wouldn't share with the cultural office their personal testimonies of how they were raised, or legends, or family stories—things that needed to be preserved or put on record in some way—they shared that with me orally.

Working there sixteen years, sharing their stories and their heartaches, put me in a very unique position. The directorship of this office opened when what I always call the horse-and-buggy seniors were passing away. With their passing, there wasn't much more I could learn about the old life. So when this job opened, I applied for it, in hopes that some day I'd be able to play a part in passing on those teachings that otherwise might be lost to our people.

So I worked with the 4-H people on their camp, and this year we had about a half-and-half camp. We taught the 4-H stuff, but with a cultural twist. We put language in there, legends, stories, dance and song, plant identification. Probably one of the most overwhelming things, which gives me great pride when I talk about it, is when I decided to teach them some of our social dances, dances that we do only for our own people, not like powwow dancing.

I took my drum, and I taught them how to dance. The little kids, the third- and fourth-grade kids, ate it up. I taught them how to do the dance, and I sang the song. We did that one night, and then the next night, and before we even had our campfire, the kids were already all around asking me if I was going to bring my drum out again. When I told them yes, they got excited about it.

We had the campfire, and we danced. One of the teachings a long time ago was that when you learn to recognize the song, no one has to tell you what the dance is going to be. When the singer starts singing, you jump up and start doing what needs to be done. By the third day, the third- and fourth-graders were doing that on their own. I'd just start the song, and they'd line up and do what they needed to do. It was amazing.

I added on a new dance every evening, and by the end, all the kids were anxious to dance. The little guys have their apprehensions about holding hands with boys, and especially with girls, but as they got into the spirit of the dance and started to learn the song and help me sing, they forgot about their fears.

Then we got the older kids. Some of them went up there to see their little brothers or sisters and ended up in the second week of camp. These were fifth- and sixth-grade age. That age group was a little more difficult to work with, but with the help of the staff, I was able to do it.

We got all the kids to participate in the dancing and singing. I told a different legend every night, and whenever I told a legend, it just got quiet around the camp fire. They really listened.

That happened in July of this year, and this is November now, and I still see kids on the street—and the 4-H staff people see them too—who come up and ask, "When are we going to have a dance?" or "When is Wilson going to tell legends?" "Are we going to have a camp next year?" That makes me feel good inside in my heart. Our kids are hungry for that kind of teaching.

On the last day of the camp we had an open house for both groups. We invited the little kids with their families to come back for a salmon bake. We had some of our Tribal Council people there. Parents and grandparents came. Things were winding down, and kids were loading up and getting ready to head out. I didn't know if I could pull it off or not, but I told the kids that on the open house day, I wanted them to dance and sing just the way they had been doing, without being ashamed of what their parents or anybody else thought about it. I told them to forget about that. "Show them what you've learned," I told them. "Don't be ashamed to dance, because this is our dance. Don't be ashamed to sing, because the song belongs to you. I taught you guys how to be brothers and sisters—not boys and girls, but brothers and sisters. Have fun just like you had fun with me all these two weeks."

On the day of the open house, I told the co-director, "Well, I guess it's time to see if the kids are going to show what they've learned about the dances and songs." I went to my pickup and reached behind the seat, and I got my drum out and shut the door, and some of the boys over by their camp saw me getting my drum, and they ran up, excited: "We gonna dance?" "Yep," I told them.

There's a way that you call people to get ready for the dance. You hit the drum three times. I hit the drum once, and the co-director's husband was walking from the other end of the camp, and he heard the drum hit, and he told me later, "Before you even hit it the second time, there were kids running from tipis and tents and from down by the creek and from out by the KP tent. They were running from everywhere before you hit the drum the second time. By the third time they were already getting in line, and when you started singing, they were all lined up right behind you singing too."

We went into the open place in the camp there, and we started the dance, and the parents and grandparents gathered around. I almost cried because the kids put on a very wonderful dance. They sang and danced, and they conducted themselves in a really good manner. Afterwards some of the parents came and asked me, "How the heck did you ever get my kid to participate? We can't even drag him to a powwow, and he was out there throwing his arms around and jumping off the ground. How did you get my kid singing Indian songs?"

The songs I sang at the camp were put on a tape by some of our elders a long time ago, in the seventies. But there comes a time when the kids start relating a song to the person who taught it to them. So I had to make a tape of the same songs that our elders sang, and they play it on the radio every now and then. The kids hear me singing on there, and their parents or grandparents tell me, "They hear your voice come on the radio, and pretty soon they're moving like they're ready to dance, but if you look at them, they don't dance. But if we pretend we're not paying attention, then they get into the motion and dance right in the living room." And they say, "That's really a change in the child."

The opportunity for me to be the director and introduce all this into the curriculum in the grade school or the middle school or the high school is what I want. Right now I have a request from the middle school to fill eight dates with speakers. Eight forty-five-minute talks. They have an Indian literature class at the middle school, and I've never met the teacher, but I think she has a good heart, because she says that she hasn't found any literary material that she feels is suitable to teach the Indian kids. She wants somebody to come from here to talk about things that the Indian kids can identify with. That's the reason for the eight spots during the nine-week period. I'm going to take two dates; I have another guy who's going to take two; our language teacher's going to take one; the governmental affairs office will probably take one. That's going to be somewhat of a pilot program, and if we're able to increase the kids' knowledge of Indian affairs as a result of the Indian literature class, and they retain what we teach them, then it will make one more avenue to introduce something worthwhile into the curriculum, something that's relevant to the kids.

I'm also involved in a project with Oregon State University. They're helping me by compiling information from various sources for the section of their library that's concerned only with Warm Springs. They're collecting recordings, written records, all they can get, and once that's compiled, I'll go down there, and we'll start going through all the material and make a chronological history. My dream is that we'll make a history that will finally turn into a textbook for the tribes to use at some level of teaching our children. We can break it down into some introductory stuff for grade school and go on from there. It's important to start early. Right now, with our grade-school kids, and even at our early childhood center (which is a Head Start and day care center), we'll go over there and tell legends and sing songs for them.

We're introducing those things into the school, and hopefully it will work. It's my thought that if we start giving back to our children a sense of identity, we'll start making them proud of what they are. When you start taking ownership of your identity, start being proud of the legends of your people, proud of the history of the reservation, proud of the songs and dances, all the cultural aspects, then I think it's just like with language. There are studies that show that if language is made a part of an indigenous group's academic learning, the group excels in other areas of study. Hawaiians have done that, and we can too. If we give our young people back their cultural identity, then they can succeed in learning what direction to take their lives. Some of them might go on to higher education in some field of study that could help develop the tribes further, something to help give our people back that decision-making power that was taken away from them long ago.

I think, in a way, that's what happens at the culture camp with the boys. Today you have children growing up ashamed of how they look. I took the boys to go sweat up in the mountains. A lot of the boys had never sweated before; they didn't know what a sweat house was; they didn't know how to prepare. I walked them through that whole process.

When we went there, a lot of them undressed only down to a certain point. Some of them brought swimming trunks, and I told them, "That's not our way here." So while I had them together there by the creek, I talked to them about being proud of who they are, proud of their bodies. We're all created differently, and there's no reason to be ashamed of being tall and skinny or short and fat, or light-complected or dark-complected, or any other thing that has to do with our bodies. We were there for a purpose, and that was to cleanse our bodies inside and out and acknowledge one another as brothers—not to look at one another as being Warm Springs, Wasco, or Paiute. We even had some white boys up there.

They felt more comfortable after I talked to them that way. They took off the rest of their stuff until they were completely naked, and they took turns getting in the sweat house. We made sweat house twice a day, and after the first day, it was nothing for them to come and strip and be prepared to go in. It was just that nobody had ever taught them those things before. I couldn't be down there when the girls were down there, but I did talk to the elder ladies and some of the women that were helping to teach. I told them what I taught the boys. I told them, "There's going to be girls that are shy like that, too, and you can teach them not to be ashamed of their bodies."

I also told the boys they were going to find out later that girls are different from us. They're not made the same. But you don't make fun of the girls because they're girls, because we have more to our anatomy than they do. Think of them as your sisters. If they're younger, then they're little sisters; if they're older, then they're big sisters. I asked the boys if they'd want anybody to talk ugly to their moms, call their mom things. They all shook their heads. "Well," I told them, "your mom's a girl too. If you talk bad to a girl, then you're talking like that to your own mom."

Every night at the camp fire, I asked the boys, "Okay, what are these girls to you?" "Our sisters," they said. "And you girls, what are these boys to you?" "That's our brothers." They got along without fighting or calling names. I think everybody that visited the camp found that the traditional teaching helped our children.

One of the things that happened up there was that we went on an overnight camp-out. Prior to the camp-out, before the Fourth of July, the family of one boy who was there had sold fireworks up in Washington. So this boy had made some income for himself. He put it in his tent, and it got taken. The boys who were at the camp at that time got punished; they were told to stay in that area and not to participate in activities.

When I got back to camp, I was told what had happened, and it distressed me enough so that I got the boys together to talk about it. I told them, "You know I tried to teach you guys something good up here, to respect one another. And now this money is gone, and it hurts me, because it means I didn't teach you in a good way. I don't know who took it, but I'm going to put a box on my pickup, and I hope that wallet will come back. I don't want to know who took it; I don't want to know anything. The person who took that wallet—you're going to live with that the rest of your life. You're going to always know that you came to this camp for a good thing, and then you did that. It will always be with you, always haunt you; it will eat away at you forever. You'll never be able do get rid of it. Maybe after doing this thing you'll do other bad things, get worse. I'm trying to help you so you'll do better for yourself."

That night was the last night of camp, and I'd already bought a bunch of marshmallows, all the contraband that you ban during the duration of the camp but save to give them a treat, a good send-off. I was going to withhold it, but then I thought about the teaching of my grandma. She said, "When you get something for somebody, even if that person doesn't know about it, if you decide to withhold it, you're doing wrong."

So I went and got all that stuff, and I brought it to camp and got all the boys together and told them what my grandma taught me—that when you get something for somebody you don't ever take it back. I told them, "I didn't want you guys to have this because of the theft that took place, but I'm not the one that has to live with that. Whoever did that wrong thing has to live with it. You guys have your party, have fun tonight."

I left and headed back to my tipi. I was getting ready to go to bed and went down to the creek, and then came back and went into my tipi and was ready to go to sleep, when I thought, "Well, I guess I'd better check that box before I go to bed." I got up and went out, and the wallet was there.

I went and told the co-director, and then I went to the boys and told them, "This wallet has been returned, and the money's in it. That makes me feel real happy inside." I cried standing there. I said, "You guys have fun. Whoever it is who returned this, you'll always, always remember this day; even if you turn the wrong way in your life, you can always look back at this day and know you did something good."

A lot of our kids don't get the teaching they need. I'm only one man, but I know there are lot of people in our community who have knowledge to teach our children. This year we're going to try to get more resource people up there at camp, more tribal people. One aspect that I didn't mention was that last year there was a hunger for the spiritual part. This year we're going to add more of our spiritual teachings. Maybe we'll include something every morning, even before breakfast, because that's a good time. That's probably going to happen this year, so that all the kids can learn about our religion. It will start to become ingrained in them. If they start getting interested in it, hopefully that interest will be nurtured by their parents. If the kids can go back and share with their parents, maybe the parents will even come to this office and ask about a program for adults. Our community can start to heal. I think we can win our kids back. I know we can.

After our interview, in an adjoining room, Wilson demonstrated a computer program designed to help Warm Springs children learn their native languages. When a screen displayed a raccoon, or a raven, or a deer, or a salmon, or a coyote, the name of the creature was spelled out in both English and Sahaptin, Paiute, or Wasco; and a voice pronounced the native word clearly.

It seems fitting that an extension of the technology that helped destroy native cultures should also serve to recall and preserve them.

Wilson Wewa Jr.

Stoney Miller

Avex D. "Stoney" Miller, born and raised on the reservation, was recently named chief of the Warm Springs Police Department. The interview was conducted in his office. (At a few minutes before 10 A.M., in the waiting room outside near the green metal door to the jail, a mother arrived with clean underwear for her son in his cell. Underpants were allowed in, but the T-shirts she had brought were turned away by the secretary in charge. As the mother left, a young man arrived to check on his stolen rifle, which hadn't been recovered.)

Stoney Miller (AUTHOR PHOTO)

I've worked fourteen years with this department out of a total of twenty-three years in law enforcement. My dad served sixteen or eighteen years on the Tribal Council back in the forties and fifties.

As for education, I was in the group that went through just when the boarding schools were finishing here. That would be in the mid-sixties. There were a lot of ill feelings over those boarding schools. The discipline there was very severe at times. Kids had to live there, so they never got to know their families very well. There was a strong push back then to get away from tribal languages and speak English all the time. Nobody was ever allowed to talk Indian at school or in the dormitory.

I hear comments every once in a while about our law here versus the white man's law. Part of that comes about because of what we have to do at the police academy. My officers here attend the Oregon Police Academy, just like the officers from anywhere else. They go through the same nine weeks of intensive training as anybody else in the state.

So one problem is that everything at the academy is oriented toward state law—traffic, criminal, everything else is geared to Oregon statutes. But we have our own codes here. Our traffic code and criminal code are adopted by the Tribal Council. Actually, they're written pretty much as paraphrases of the state codes, but they aren't the same. We don't have a book of traffic laws that would be this big (he holds up a book about two inches thick). Ours would be about a third the size of this.

But it isn't true that we're trying to get away from white man's laws. The officers here at Warm Springs have traditionally had to work with a number of types of law. We've got our tribal law and order code, traffic code, and criminal code that we work with all the time. We also have to be acquainted with state law and, to a degree, with county ordinances. Beyond that, we also have to have an awareness of federal law. Some of our officers spend a lot of their own time going through books to increase their legal knowledge.

This idea of us getting away from anything—or getting away *with* anything—just isn't true. I've heard that said though, a number of times. I've worked for other agencies, including the Malheur County Sheriff's Office, where I spent a good number of years as a resident deputy. I remember when I was interviewed there, the sheriff asked me what kind of law we worked with up here. When I explained all this to him, he was impressed with the fact

Stoney Miller

that we had so many different kinds of things to work with and worry about.

So part of the attitude about us is based on the fact that other people don't really understand what we do. Part of it's based on prejudices. And some of it has to do with the sovereignty issue. We do have full sovereignty on this reservation. At a place like Umatilla, the state and the tribes operate on a concurrent jurisdiction, which means the state has authority within the reservation boundaries up there. Sovereignty is something that Warm Springs has never given up.

Over the years, we've been accused of favoritism when it comes to our treatment of people accused of committing crimes outside the reservation. To a degree, there is some truth to that. If a tribal member has a warrant from some other jurisdiction outside, before we can serve that warrant here, we have to get it authorized by a tribal judge. We can take a copy of the warrant and walk it across the street to the chief tribal judge. If she feels that this person needs to make atonement for whatever the offense was, she'll sign the warrant, and then we can serve on the individual. We pick him up and make arrangements to get him into the county system. It's a drawn-out process, and it does create some headaches.

We don't have to go through quite so many hoops on federal warrants. If an individual is arraigned in federal court and a warrant is issued, or an indictment is issued, those can be served without the tribal judge's signature. Federal stuff is usually more serious. Over the years going back to the middle seventies, when I started working for this department, I can remember some instances when we had individuals running around here who had state warrants, but we couldn't enforce them. It was either because the judge back then wouldn't sign off on the thing, or somebody else somewhere in the hierarchy didn't want them served.

Over the past three years, I've been a captain, and then I stepped up to the position I'm in now. I've spent a lot of that time working on firming up relations with other agencies. We work with the Oregon State Police a lot now, especially the game officers on the north side over here. If one of them needs assistance and one of our game officers is in the area, our man will go across and give a hand.

There's an area called Rock Creek on ceded lands north of the reservation. The group of people living there was seen as militant by the Wasco County Sheriff's Office. They weren't complying with Forest Service rules and regulations. The sheriff asked us to give them a hand, and I spent some extra time working with the folks up at Rock Creek, getting acquainted with them. Then at one of our joint agency meetings, I talked to the Forest Service personnel about the fact that they needed to change their approaches a little bit. They needed to learn some traditional ways to communicate with these Rock Creek folks and alleviate some of the hostility and aggressiveness that had built up over the years.

The Forest Service people took my suggestions. That particular day when I mentioned it, we were on our way up to Rock Creek to meet with the folks, and three of the Forest Service people went with us. We got there and went over, and after I introduced everybody, I just kind of backed out of the scene and let these folks just visit. That changed their whole communication pattern. Before that, the Forest Service would go up there to see these folks and just hop out of their vehicle and tell them, "We need you to do this, and do it now." All they needed to do was be social and visit a little bit—not about anything specific, just visit. Spend some time there, and then bring up your business. They started doing that, and now they haven't had any conflicts for a year and a half.

I've known the man who's sheriff of Jefferson County now for a number of years, and we've worked together on a lot of things. We get along great. The chief of police in Madras was chief here for a year and a half, so this is the first time Madras has had a chief who's acquainted with how we do things out here on the reservation.

In the last five years, there have been seven chiefs of police here. Sometimes people come in and work a year, a year and a half, and then move on to somewhere else. A tribal member who was chief ran into some personal family problems. A couple of people were just temporary. We've had several non-tribal members as police chiefs, but there's a lot of pressure on any who comes in here to take this position. You have to be open minded, and you have to be able to communicate. You have to go out and talk to folks on a one-

Stoney Miller

on-one basis. For somebody who doesn't really know the people here, it's tough.

I feel comfortable in the job because for the last two, two and a half years, I've spent a lot of time going out and visiting with people one-on-one. I've caught heck about things that have happened here; I've been chewed out about calls that weren't answered and cases that weren't followed up on. I listen to these people and let them chew my ear. When they're done, I give them answers. If I don't have an answer, I tell them I'll find one and get back to them. Then we have some friendly conversation about things in general. That way, I get to know their feelings, and they find out about my concerns. I take some of their ideas and incorporate them into what we provide as services. You have to work at getting along with people. The way I look at police work, we can't do an effective job on our side if we don't get some help and some input from the citizenry. We sure as heck can't do our jobs well if they don't give us some help, if we don't communicate.

The last I heard, we have about forty-three hundred people here on the reservation. The average age is fairly young, and most of the complaints I get are about juveniles and kids a little older. A lot of it's vandalism, graffiti, window breaking, that kind of stuff. Television and movies have something to do with it. The parents have something to do with it, too. We had a generation here that didn't adopt some of the discipline and culture from the past. A lot of parents just don't pay attention to their kids. But that's been true in a lot of places in the world for the past ten or twenty years.

We have some statistics that were prepared just about a year ago. For Indian country—reservations all around the United States—juvenile delinquency and gang activity, criminal activity, violence, there had been an increase of over 47 percent in I think just a two-year span. Talking with people I know on other reservations, it sounds like a lot of it stems from the same things we've got here. For a while parents just stopped caring about what their kids were doing. The family structure wasn't there. A lot of these kids, if they don't have a family structure to relate to, they get involved with gangs. Then they belong to something; they get some prestige. Supposedly somebody cares about them.

There are some really sad-looking figures from the Southwest, the Navajos, Apaches, and Hopis. Homicides and manslaughters have gone up something like 80 percent in this two-year period. If you really look at all this, police agencies are so badly undermanned that they can't begin to get a handle on problems like those.

We have that situation here. We've got eleven officers for patrol, and we're down to one officer for fish and game, instead of four. We should have ten people back there on our corrections staff, and we have seven. It's a constant go-round. One of our biggest problems, as far as keeping manpower is concerned, is the wages. We're one of the lowest-paid agencies in the state. What often happens is, we hire people who aren't Indian, and we get them trained, and then they move on somewhere else. We're paying a patrolman $19,273 a year, starting wages, and that same guy can go to one of the counties and jump up to $24, $26, $27,000 a year. If he's got a family to take care of, there's no way I can blame him for leaving here.

The non-Indian officers who do stay aren't staying for the money. It's because they care about the people here. They like the community, and they like the reservation. I have to remind our people of that sometimes. We have Indians from other tribes here too, and some of our people even look at them as non-Indians.

If I was lucky enough to go down here and have the Tribal Council tell me that they were approving the funding for hiring and equipping eighteen more people, I could take those people and spread them out through the department here in the different divisions, and that would make a big difference. But we do have some positive things. We have more certified officers than we've ever had before. We've got officers committed to staying here and working at making things better. These officers are always coming up with new ideas, new things to try.

Our investigation staff is undermanned, just like the rest of the department, but the investigators we do have are always pushing to get stuff done. We could use more, but overall we've got better equipment than we've ever had before. A couple of years ago the Tribal Council gave us some extra money, so 95 percent of our officers have protective vests. At one time, the only ones who had them were the ones who bought them out of their own pockets.

At one time, I was the only certified instructor in the entire department. That was for firearms. Right now we've got five people here who are certified instructors in different fields, more than we've ever had before. Two years ago I started a program I'm still working on, to try to develop instructors in certain select areas. That will give us three advantages. One, when we get these people certified as instructors, it builds their credibility within the community, and also in court. Number two, we won't have to send people away, like we've always had to do, for training. And number three, we have the training available right here for sensitive issues, maybe in the way something's handled out on the street, such as the use of force. Right now we have two gentlemen here, one detective and one patrolman, who are certified use-of-force instructors. If the Tribal Council has a question about how something was done, these guys can take their books, their tapes, and all their training files down to the council, and they can demonstrate right there in the council chambers why something was done and how it was taught—they can lay the whole thing out. Before, if something like that came up, we always had to rely on somebody coming in from an outside agency to explain.

When I started in law enforcement, it was back in the transition days—the days when some of the old-timers, if they were interrogating somebody and didn't get the answers they were looking for, it wasn't uncommon to see a knee put into a stomach. You can't do that stuff now. But I broke in with some of those types of officers and learned some good and some bad from them. I saw law enforcement change to the day of the trained officer.

Historically, in general council meetings the police department has been one of the major topics of discussion, and most of the comments were negative. But this last fall, at two general council meetings that were held, there were no really negative comments made about the police department. There were actually a number of positive remarks made about us. I took that as a big step forward.

I write as a sort of stress reliever. I started getting interested in writing back in grade school. I wrote stories in several of my classes. I kept it up through junior high and high school. At college— I went to Oregon Institute of Technology at Klamath Falls—I wrote a number of short stories and technical articles for my classes. My folks had instilled an appreciation for books in me. I always spent a lot of time reading. I still do, and it bugs my wife at times, because when I do have free time, I usually have my face buried in a book.

A while back, about two years ago, I hadn't done any of my own writing at all for a long time. And I just couldn't get my work done here in the office. Finally, I just quit trying to get anywhere on my office work. I started doing my own writing instead, and I finished a story. Then, when I went back to my office project, I could do it again. I went right through and finished what I'd been having all the trouble on.

Now, whenever I get bogged down really bad, I just shut it down. I spend maybe thirty minutes or an hour on my own writing, and then I'll go back to my office work, and I can accomplish something.

My mother had a hand in my writing interests. She did her own writing, and I really wish she would have left it behind. She had diaries that she kept for years, but she destroyed all of it before she passed away.

My grandfather on my dad's side was one of very few men from this reservation who made his living on the outside back then. All the years my dad was in grade school and high school, Grandpa worked for a ranch out of Prineville. My dad was the only Indian kid in Crook County schools at that time.

Grandpa Miller was on a number of trail drives back into Kansas, Missouri, Illinois—one of them went to New Orleans. His life-style was different from most of the other Indian people around here. He lived in both worlds before very many people were doing it.

I have one son who lives over toward Kah-Nee-Ta. My oldest son is in Gulfport, Mississippi, in the navy. I have a boy working over in Portland. I have a son up by Pendleton, and his twin sister has been living with me for the past year. I've got a daughter who lives over in Idaho. I'm taking her back home this afternoon. This is her right here (indicates the photo of a lovely young woman on a shelf behind his desk). She's been playing the fiddle for about three years now. She was over here on her spring break, and she did performances at Kah-Nee-Ta and at the senior center and a number of

Stoney Miller

other places. They recorded her at the radio station. I've been married and divorced several times; that's why the kids are scattered around like that. Part of that I attribute to the law enforcement career.

These last three years I've been averaging I guess about eleven hours a day down here at work, and sometimes it's fifteen, sixteen hours, depending on what I'm working on. A lot of times during the day, I don't get accomplished what I need to, so I stay after work to get caught up. That takes its toll after a while.

My mother was in law enforcement for eighteen years, with Jefferson County. Then she spent almost three years out here working for the tribal police department. When I was a kid, I was well acquainted with the lifestyle. My dad was a brand inspector, the first true brand inspector the reservation ever had. He wrote the first brand book for livestock owners. He had a federal commission and worked on a lot of cases. Growing up around that, between he and my mother, I knew what law enforcement was like.

I thought real hard about that stuff. I remembered when we'd have plans to do something, and then dad would get called out on a case and wasn't able to go, or else mom and I were going to be doing something, and she'd have to go back to work. I knew what law enforcement was before I ever got into it.

When I talk about tracking, I mean the ability to follow signs and tell where a person or animal went. I must have been four or five years old when my dad started teaching me that. He started me out when we'd be riding for cattle. He'd put me on a track, and then he'd take off and then catch up with me after a while and see if I was still on it. He was real strict about that stuff. If I was on the wrong track, I'd get smacked in the leg usually, and he'd put me on another track to try again.

After a while, I did start to see the specifics. When I got older, he started teaching me how to track people. I'd never been to a true tracking school until 1990, and when I went there I got some ideas, but the basic elements were what I'd learned from my dad forty years ago.

There's a lot to it. Following footsteps of a person is literally a step-by-step process. We work with a tracking stick, which is three or four feet long, with two or three rubber bands on it. The first rubber band on the handle end is the heel, the second one is the toe, and the third one is the heel again. That gives you the length of the foot and the stride length.

If you get into an area where you aren't really seeing any prints, that's where that stick comes into play. When you're sweeping it back and forth and watching the tip, your eye will pick up a tiny scratch on a leaf, or some dust that's transferred off of grass or left on grass, or it might be some dew that's knocked off. It might be a little twig that's bent over. Basically, you learn to look for any kind of disruption of your ground, your grasses, your weeds, dirt, or rocks.

I've tracked a lot of people on search work—missing persons, missing hunters, children. I've also tracked in a lot of criminal cases. Probably the oldest criminal case I ever worked on originated over in Idaho. There was an incident with a drug informant who had disappeared. It had been almost an exact year since the time this girl had disappeared until the sheriff's department had come up with some information on where her body might be.

They had been out into the crime scene area on a Wednesday, I think it was, and that evening they contacted me and asked me if I could be over there the next morning. When I got there the next morning, they briefed me on what their suspect had told them.

They'd been out there in late fall, during rain storms and such, and both guys involved had been wearing tennis shoes. Both of them were fairly big guys—two hundred and twenty, two hundred and thirty pounds. One of the suspects painted a kind of a picture of where they'd taken the girl, stabbed her, and thrown her off a cliff. Then they'd gone down to the base of the cliff and tried to slit her throat. Then they went to a small creek and washed up. She'd crawled off, and they chased her down in the dark and threw some rocks on her and tried to cave her head in. Then they'd climbed a hill back up to the road.

After getting briefed on this series of events and looking the ground over, I decided that instead of trying to follow it from the beginning through the end, I'd go up and walk the road. I tried to put myself into a mental picture of what these guys had been looking at when they did this crime. It had been nighttime, and they were coming up out of a rocky draw. On this road bank there were only two places that weren't overgrown completely with brush.

I went down through the widest spot, because I figured that's what they would have seen out there in the dark. I worked my way down that hill, cutting along the hillside for sign. After about an hour, I found my first footprint. The age on it was just about right for a year, and it had remnants of a tennis shoe sole pattern on one edge. The foot had stepped and slipped in the mud on the hillside, and on the bottom edge was just a little bit left of that sole pattern, and there was also just a tiny bit at the top edge.

I marked that and I kept working my way down the hillside. It took me several hours, and in that time I found two more footprints. They were old and pretty much deteriorated for tread design, but they were the right shape, right size, right age.

When I got down to the bottom, I skirted around where they'd located the girl's body, and then I picked out another area where I would have walked if I was out there in the dark. I came up with some more footprints, which eventually took me on a back trail right to the creek. One guy had left his jacket lying on the ground that night after he washed the blood off at the creek. The jacket was still there. I backtracked from there to the cliff where the girl had been thrown off. I found some scuff marks on the moss where her body had scraped. Down on the ground I found some hair fibers that turned out to be hers.

Finally I ended up back on top of the cliff, and I'd flagged out all these footprints and different bits of evidence I'd found. I gave the sheriff and chief deputy a good, clear picture of where all these different things had taken place.

You can tell all kinds of things about people by their footprints. You can tell if they've had leg or foot injuries; you can tell if they're walking just to sightsee, or if they're trying to get away from something. You can tell if they're relaxed or if they're panicked. You develop the art to the point where you can tell a right-handed rider from a left-handed rider on a horse.

When my dad was teaching me when I was a kid, his line of thinking was that when I could get to where I could track something like a squirrel or a mouse out of the brush, then I'd be a tracker. I finally achieved that when I was fifteen. I had a buddy of mine along, and we'd spotted a squirrel coming down off a tree and going off through the brush. I told my partner to stay where he was and watch for that squirrel, and I'd go down and see if could pick up its track and follow it. I followed that thing back to the tree, and my partner told my dad about it. So I passed my test with a witness who could verify it.

I've been involved in a number of search operations where we found the victims alive. I've been in plenty when the victims were deceased. We have several people living here on the reservation who are excellent trackers. Besides me, there are Vincent Macey, Marcia Macey—they're brother and sister—and Susy Macey, who's Vincent's wife. Keith Baker, who lives over here, is non-Indian, but he's married to an Indian lady, and he's a good tracker. There are others.

We run a cadet program, and most of the kids in there are involved in search and rescue work. One of my daughters and several of the other cadets have achieved very high levels of skill in tracking.

Tracking almost fits in the realm of lost arts. Through history, tracking was used for two things: either locating food, or locating enemies. The references are always to scouts or trackers. With the pioneers moving west, trackers found the game to supply the food. In the Indian wars, the scouts were the ones who found out where the enemies were.

Everything kind of faded away for a while in the early 1900s. Things were coming to an end. Then, in about 1920, tracking was used to find bootleggers and illegal immigrants. The U.S. Border Patrol went into using tracking along the borders. From that point, it progressed up to the early sixties, when there was an incident in California when a little girl disappeared. There'd been a search going for her for over a week, with several hundred people looking for this girl.

If I remember right, there were two border patrol agents from Chula Vista, California, who'd been reading the newspaper accounts of the search. These guys got clearance to go up and get involved with the search, and they talked to the people in charge and went to work on it. It took them just about twenty-four hours to find that little girl. She was suffering from exposure and dehydration, but she was still alive. That was one of the first well-known uses of tracking for search and rescue work.

From that point, some of the search and rescue organizations in California, and the border patrol, started exchanging information and developing tracking as an art for search and rescue work. It was either 1974 or '78 when the Oregon Council of Search and Rescue began using tracking as a tool. They started holding classes to teach search and rescue people how to track. That's how it progressed up to what we have today.

To me, tracking is kind of a dual-purpose thing. I grew up learning it from one of the elders. Some of the old-timers I grew up around, that were my dad's age or older, they did it all the time when they were working cattle or horses, or when they were hunting. I'm happy that it's definitely something that's related back to Indians in history.

Some of our trackers here at Warm Springs, myself included, have been invited into other areas to share our expertise. We conduct classes and training, and we're also used as a last resort on search operations.

I had an incident in Wheeler County five years ago. There was a cowboy over there who disappeared. His horse was found, and his dog turned up, but there wasn't any sign of the cowboy. I knew the sheriff over there, and he called me late one evening and wanted to know if I could put together a team and be over there the next morning by four o'clock. I went ahead and got things cleared and got a team formed.

I think there were eleven of us that went over. Nine or ten of us were trackers at different skill levels, and one guy was along for support. We met with the sheriff's department, and they briefed us on where the guy's horse had turned up and where his dog had turned up. We went out on the field there, and not quite forty minutes after we got started, we found the man's body. That turned into a homicide investigation. He had a bullet through his chest. From what I saw, I could tell he'd come down a hill and got off his horse and taken a few steps, and then he was shot. That investigation's still pending. I just talked to the sheriff over there two days ago, and they've just come up with some new leads on the case.

A number of years ago we had a couple of our trackers go over to Idaho to help on a case in the Salmon Wilderness country. A lady had disappeared out there. I wanted to go, but I couldn't get away then, so I sent two people who I thought were good enough. They spent four days over there, but they never did find her body.

But our team here at Warm Springs has a very high ratio of what we call live finds. That's how the good ones turn out.

EXCERPTS FROM STONEY MILLER'S WRITINGS

The spirits are in the wind yearning for one
To pause, take time and learn to listen.
I am one of the people of this land.
Our lives are guided by Grandfather above,
The earth beneath us, our Grandmother.
Knowledge is gained through our elders
As they learned from theirs over time.

This great land of ours has many such places, Sacred Ground.
This honor is given to these places for many reasons,
A ridge top where a boy made his first kill,
A valley where the old ones fought their battles.

The old ones gave their beliefs and skills,
Sign-cutting skills that could track a mouse,
What was needed to survive in wilderness,
The ability to communicate with our surroundings,
Speak with creatures of the land and learn from them,
To take what is needed but not abuse that which is not.
Grandfather will give the guidance needed,
And during times it is needed the strength to go on.
Of these teachings come the ways of talking,
Speaking to spirits and the wind, finding Sacred Ground.

Once on a lonely starlit night I stood listening to coyotes
Off far in the distance crooning their shrill chorus.

Stoney Miller

Shadows cast by the darkness as the moon crept
Gave off an eerie sense of foreboding in a land of great distance.
Cows bawled here and there as the heat faded,
And the sharp whistles of birds echoed in the fading light.

The experience of riding in the winter is unique, known only
To the ones who have been there in the saddle, feeling the wind.
To have grown up doing this was nothing new or special,
But now reflections bring to mind winter winds,
The feeling of stirrups stiff from cold, fingers the same,
Switching hands, warming one inside the chaps, then the other,
The numbing of fingers, toes, cheeks and nose.

Another time we were bringing a wild bunch to Beaver Trap,
Timber horses, half crazy and loco wild, running full tilt,
Only to find the damn corral gate closed,
So the horses came to a sudden stop and turned.
If there's one place you don't want to be with wild horses,
It's in front of them when they turn.
I pulled King up to a slide, spun him around and kicked.
We started to go but too late, the lead horse hit us,
Knocking us down, spinning us around, and over us they came.

King came to his end when he got caught in a cattle guard.
He was held tight and the day wore on.
As the hours passed he developed a sweat, then a chill.
When they finally pulled him out he could barely stand.
He lay on fresh hay in the barn,
And when I got home he was turning sick with fever.
We did all we could, shots of Combiotic and blankets.
I sat with him through the night, rubbing his limbs.
In the early hours of the morning he went off
To where the grass grows greener,
But in my mind he's still in the hills.
I've heard him nicker, talking to me at times.

Warm Springs Millennium

Lillian Brunoe

Lillian Brunoe, 39, is the proprietor of Sidaikba Native Collectables at Warm Springs Plaza. ("Sidaikba" translates into "special place," "precious place," or "something sacred.") She has lived on the reservation since 1986. Her husband Cecil is Wasco and a Warm Springs tribal member.

Lillian Brunoe (AUTHOR PHOTO)

In 1985 I was up in Washington at a place called Port Angel selling Ford cars. Then I met a friend from Warm Springs who had heard I was up in Washington. He went up there to ask me if I would come down to Warm Springs and check out the place where he lives. He was trying to get a survival school together. [A survival school is an alternative for children who aren't happy with public schools.] He'd found out that I wrote proposals and knew how to talk to people and get them to donate things for different causes and so on, because that's what I used to do. I'd done national economic development in California for six years. I helped with the Red Wind Foundation, which is a Native American community. I did housing and cattle and all that kind of stuff. So I had a track record, and they found out I was up there and went out of their way to get me.

I was born in San Diego and brought up in California. I was raised in the mountains at the Red Wind Foundation. We had no electricity, only wood-burning stoves and kerosene light. We lived off the land and had a traditional, ceremonial lifestyle. A lot of different tribes were involved. I'm Apache-Yaqui on my mom's side and Aztec Indian on my dad's side. We still do our traditions on both sides, the Aztec dances and ceremonies and the Apache and Yaqui ceremonies too.

Back when I was twenty-five years old, I decided to leave the Red Wind Foundation and go away to school. I went to Palomar College near San Diego and then up to Questa College at San Luis Obispo. I wanted to learn about the law and education—get more of a handle on society, I guess—to be able to help the non-profit organizations. It was difficult, at the age of twenty-five, making that transition from living off the land—the wood-burning stoves, kerosene light, no stoplights to go across the street, all of that.

It was really different. I was a single woman with four children, and we lived in a little Mazda station wagon for three months before we could even get a house to live in. We went through a really rough time. We lived in that car for three months, even though I had three thousand dollars saved up just to make the move. But nobody would rent a house to a single woman with four kids.

I finally got a place, and it was like the Creator helped me out. I was at a pizza place with my little kids, and a lady came up to me and said, "You know, I'm leaving for Los Angeles, and I've been watching you all evening, the way you are with your children, and I admire you. I want to know if you can take care of my house plants." I told her I'd love to, but that I was living in my car. So she said, "Why don't you live in my house? It still has rent for a month, and you can get ahold of the landlord." It ended up that I knew the landlord from the Red Wind Foundation. We'd gone through a big uranium scare and had to fight the corporations to leave the Indians alone. We won the case, and I got to know the forestry guys, so I ended up living in a house that was owned by one of them.

I decided to go to college and ended up helping create a women's resource center. I helped them get a shelter home together. We had to deal with the city councils on both sides of the hill, but we got our shelter home. We got a lot of teenagers off the streets, and we created a dial-a-teen organization where if a senior citizen or somebody needed some work done, they called, and a teen would go and help. It worked really well, and I was getting popular in the community. But then I got tired of all the politics, so I ended up selling Kirby vacuum cleaners. It was from there that I went into selling cars.

I went up to Washington because a friend who was an architect wanted somebody to live in his house. I was working really hard to try to save money and buy a piece of land, and he said, "Come on over to my house, and you won't have to pay rent." So he got me the job selling cars, and we moved up there. That's when the Warm Springs people heard I was up there and decided I was supposed to be good at what I did, and they decided they wanted to bring me to Warm Springs to raise money for a survival school.

So they brought me to Warm Springs, and I got to meet the three grandmothers, the oldest people on the reservation. They told me they'd had a dream about me and already knew who I was. They had already visualized me coming here. I liked what I saw here and thought this would be a good environment for my older kids, a good place for them to go to school and live.

This was in 1986, '87. I helped with the survival school and became the teacher. My kids all went to school there. I became the school's proposal writer, their housecleaner, everything that came along. But it turned out that the community wasn't really serious enough about the school, and it got to the point where I was overwhelmed trying to do everything and be everything all by myself.

Finally I decided I might go back and sell cars and just mind my own business. But then I ended up with one of the men here, and we had three boys together. The three boys are all tribal members.

Lillian Brunoe

I really enjoy living here, being here. The people are really nice, and if you were raised like me, in the traditional ways, this is a good place, because these people do carry on their traditions.

My business is nice. I enjoy being here. I've always been a people kind of person. The way I walked into this thing was, there was a man and woman who had a little shop over on the other side of the plaza, and they were looking for someone to help, because they eventually wanted to get out of the shop. The wife wanted to go away to school. I thought helping at the store would be fun, so I talked it over with my husband. He said I could try it if I wanted to, but he wasn't real thrilled about it.

I've been doing crafts like sewing since I was fourteen years old. My mom taught me how to sew, how to weave, how to do everything. She even told me, "Someday this is going to pay off for you." I guess it did.

So finally I took over the store and enjoyed it. It was like a dream come true. I couldn't even believe it was happening. By the end of a year, I had the store so packed with merchandise that maybe only one person could fit inside. It was really small, and we did most of our on-hand sewing and leather work right there. It got to the point where people who wanted to come down and learn how to make a dress, or make moccasins, or how to bead, couldn't really fit in.

I love to teach, and the store was so small that I couldn't even put a table out to cut a dress when I needed to. The guys here where I am now, in this big shop, were going out of business, so I talked to my husband again. I told him I wanted the bigger place, that I needed the space. I wanted to teach classes, to have it so that anybody who wanted to could come down here to make jingle dresses this week, and then moccasins, and maybe dream-catchers the next week.

My overall goal is to focus on young couples, single parents, teenagers, people who are just starting off in the world, because when I was going to college, it was beadworking that got me through. That's all I did. I beaded anything and everything and never had a problem selling it. It bought the diapers, supplied the gas money, everything I needed to get me through school. I want to teach single parents, single mothers, young teenagers, that there's a way to be self-sufficient, things that can help them get through the hard times.

My older daughters, who are eighteen and sixteen, know how to make traditional outfits. They can make clothes for themselves. Just about every craft that I can do, they can do, which is nice for me too, because I can even leave them in the store.

One of my daughters is in California now going to school. The way she's been getting her money is through the beadworking. She calls me up and says, "Mom, this is awesome! I'm not poor! I can do something!"

I try to sell as many of my own things as I can in the store, but I also buy and trade from tribal members. I encourage the community to come in and be part of the store. I want this to be a place where people can feel safe, feel good about themselves. That's what I want; it's what I'm here for.

A lot of times I get people who are in that alcoholic world, drugs and drinking, and they get tired of it, but they need somewhere to go to express themselves, to feel good about themselves. I tell them, "As long as you're sober, you can always come down to the store and make something with me." It helps them. I've had different people come in and say, "I don't want to be out there anymore; I'm tired of it. Can I come here?" "Sure," I tell them, "come on, we'll make something today." And when they're done and look at what they've made, they always feel good.

I've got two different ladies starting businesses out of their own homes, making things, doing what they like to do best. I've had tribal members come in, traditional elders; all kinds of people from the community have come in here to tell me, "You're an inspiration to our tribe here. We watched you come with nothing and grow into this big beautiful shop. And you've never turned anybody away." My theory is, the more I can help, the better off we all are.

I firmly believe that the more small businesses we can get going on this reservation, the better off we'll be in the future. When society decides there's no more money, not just for Indians but for everybody, we can become self-sufficient. I'd like to see the tribe stop hiring so many outside people and start hiring their own tribal

Lillian Brunoe

members, keeping their money here. One thing that I really express to our community is that the more small businesses we have here, the better we'll connect with each other and get along. If I want my floors waxed, I want to call an Indian on the reservation who's got a cleaning service. Way too often we go to the outside world to spend our money. We have to give our own Indian people the inspiration that we can be just as good as the next people.

When I get tired of this shop, I want to see my daughters running it. I want them to have something to hold on to—our culture, our heritage, the things that we need to keep carrying on and survive as a people.

Today I was trying to get my floor mopped when a guy called me up on the phone to ask if I wanted to buy something like five hundred pens for three hundred and something dollars. I told him it sounded nice and dandy, but where was he calling from? "Oh, I'm calling from San Diego, California." So I said, "Sorry, no. I want to support my community." If I want some pens and can find some for that price here on the reservation, I'll buy them here, and if I can't find them here, then I'll go to Madras, the next nearest community. If they don't have them, then I'll try Bend.

I work hard for a living, and I'm not complaining. I'm a strong person; I can handle work, but my strong belief is to support the people around me first, and after that go to neighbors here in the state of Oregon. If more of us at Warm Springs start doing that, we will become a better nation, a stronger nation.

Most of my customers are great. I always remember this one lady who came in the store—this was when we were on the other side in the small place. She was from Japan, and she came in and had her little calculator with her. She looked at a painting, and she said, "How much?" I told her seven hundred dollars. She did something on her calculator, and then she said, "I want it for a hundred and seventy-five dollars." I told her I couldn't do that. So she went to another painting and said, "How much?" I told her three thousand dollars. She got on her calculator again. "I want it for eight hundred dollars," she said, and I told her I couldn't do that either.

Then she started looking at our jewelry, and she picked out a necklace. I said it was a two-hundred-and-fifty-dollar necklace.

 Warm Springs Millennium

This time her calculator told her she wanted it for seventy-five dollars. I looked at her, and I said, "Lady, we do everything here handmade. We sit here and we paint these paintings for days, and we sit here and we put these beads on these necklaces, and it takes us a long time to do it. I do all my own sewing here. All these things take a long, long time." "Oh," she said, "you don't buy all this stuff from Japan?"

I explained to her I didn't have anything in my store from Japan. I told her all my things were American-made, that the most American-made things you can ever get are by us Indian people. I told her she should probably go shop someplace else, so she just kind of looked at me and went off out the door. But then later she came back and said, "I really need to apologize to you. I didn't realize what I was doing."

The other day an elderly woman from Warm Springs came in with a Pendleton jacket and told me she'd just bought it from a lady in town, and it made her itch. She had some material, and she wanted me to make a lining for the jacket. I said I would and took some money for it, but when she was gone, I realized I didn't have a pattern for anything like that jacket. I had to free-hand it out, cut it all out and put it on the jacket, and when she came in and tried it on, she was satisfied. It worked, and she was happy.

Another time, a woman came in here who wanted to get married in a white man's wedding dress. She had pretty white lace, pretty white satin, black velvet to go with it, and then she had this black outer skirt material to go with it. But the pattern she had for the dress was four times too small. It was time for a reality check. We made the dress the right size and sent her to the feast.

An elderly man came in, a non-Indian, a man from Portland or someplace near there, and he was looking through all the stuff. He asked if I could make him a leather vest, and I said sure. He came back two weeks later with the leather, and I found out that it was from his own elk hunting. We measured him, and I made him an awesome vest and charged him sixty-five, seventy dollars for the job. He came back a month later and wanted another vest made for his wife, and he said, "You know, I was looking in these western catalogues from places that sell vests like this and couldn't find one for less than three hundred dollars."

Lillian Brunoe

The traditional elders come down here and sit with me, and if I show somebody how to make a dress, they show me how to make something in return. They'll sit and tell me how they made their clothes a long time ago, how they did the beadwork. Sometimes I can take their ideas and make a necklace or moccasins their way. They know they can come down here any time and ask me to do something for them, and it'll get done. It makes me feel good as a person when these people walk out of my door smiling.

The other day a man came all the way from Portland, and he said, "My mom came into this store and bought something, and she said I had to come here and look around." He looked around at this and that, and when he seemed ready to walk out the door, he'd see something else and start asking questions. Then he was ready to head out again, and the same thing happened. Finally he said he'd just have to stay a while, because he couldn't get all the way out the door.

That's what this store is for. I've had people come all the way from Arizona, New Mexico. I have a book here that people from all over the world have signed. I've had people send me a picture of something they need made, and I make it and send it back.

I enjoy my customers. Sometimes they come in and ask where the casino is, and I tell them, and then I say they should come back and spend some money after they win big. Lots of times they do. I never see any negative attitudes in here. I try to be as positive as I can be.

My twenty-two-year-old son is in college now. My sixteen-year-old daughter, Glowing Star, started school at Warm Springs in kindergarten. I think the Warm Springs Elementary School is really good. I think we need to put more tradition in our school, but that's just the way I am. I think we need to continue our Indian language classes. It would be nice to see the teachers speak more Indian than English. We should hold on to what we have.

It's really neat when my kids come home and they're talking to me in Indian. I have to say, "Wait a minute, what are you telling me?" But it's really nice, because we're all learning together. The little guys, they get a kick out of it. "Hey," they say, "we got to learn Indian language today!" I also think we should have more traditional cultural skills in our school, where they go out into the hills and do things the old way.

I don't like the schools in Madras. Madras is a joke. My daughter Glowing Star went to school there, and she hated every minute of it. The Madras school system is geared to Madras. I really don't like the idea that our children have to be taken off the reservation to go to school. They should be staying here. What really turned Glowing Star off at school was that one day she and her friends were going to a store to get a pop or something at lunch time and actually witnessed these guys with chains and bats beating somebody up.

She came home shaken and said she'd never go to school in Madras again in her life. She was determined not to go to school there. So she went to alternative school on the reservation instead. In Madras our children get exposed to a gangster lifestyle, and a lot of that, I feel, is from—and don't get me wrong; I'm not a prejudiced person and don't want to ever come across that way— but reality is reality. Madras over the years has gotten overcrowded with the Mexican-American people, and with that has come the gangsters, the idea that that's the in thing, that everybody has to wear the baggy clothes. And now it's got to the point where if you look at somebody funny, they're going to shoot you. This is ridiculous. Why do they have to send our kids off our reservation to teach them that?

Last year they took the alternative school off the reservation and put it back in Madras as part of the Madras school district. But now I've been hearing that we might build our own schools here, a middle school and a high school on the reservation. The community is 100 percent for that. Personally, I'd like to see our high school with more vocational training with things like gardening, auto mechanics, all the crafts. We could do a lot more for our children.

I have a whole different concept about education for our children. When we were young, we went to school in a one-room building, and we learned the usual things, but we also learned our traditional values. When our children have to go to Madras, they're pulled away from tradition. Our kids go into that system and learn things that have never been part of our people. Sometimes we par-

Lillian Brunoe

ents have to say to our children, "You're not Mexican; you're not black. You're Indian. You don't need the baggy clothes; you don't need to worry about who's wearing red and who's wearing black." We as parents hate that, because our Indian people have never been like that. It's a shame that that's what society has out there for our children. It's like we're cornered.

I refuse to let my younger boys wear baggy clothes and talk like they're gangsters. We go out to the hills and go camping, or we go hiking, or we go to a traditional ceremony. I believe parents need to do that; otherwise, there's not much hope for our future. Not enough people are interested in teaching true values anymore. We're not ready to get dumped in the melting pot. I was raised to believe our tradition was the most important thing in the world. Learning our dances and prayers, that's what keeps us who we are. When our children and our young adults stray away from that, we lose our identity.

Our traditional elders tell us that it's up to the younger generation to carry on traditions for our children. They say that there'll be a time when the world decides to come to an end. Only so many people will survive. Our Creator tells us that only the strong will survive, the people who hold on to their traditions and learn to live off the land, and live with the land. There's a difference between off the land and with the land. All of us human beings are living off this land. But how many of us give back to the land? We have to thank the Creator for the trees, the dirt we walk on, the plants, the air that we breathe. How many people are really giving thanks for all of that?

There's no more salmon; there's no fish in the river. It scares me to say that. What's next? No more traditional roots, no more traditional berries, no more deer meat? Worlds are colliding. The corporations are taking over the natural lives of the people. But when the world comes to an end, only the people who know how to live off the land and with the land will survive.

We partake in all the ceremonies—the huckleberry feasts, the salmon feasts, the root feasts. I'm a true believer in that. When it's time for my husband to go hunting, I tell him, "You need to sweat, to offer some tobacco or sage to the animal spirits and to the Creator. Let them know why you're out there. You're hunting to provide for your family."

When we go out to dig roots, I make sure that I make an offering or take a little bit of food to hand out to the spirits of the land. That's what I mean about living off the land and giving back to the land. That's the way I was raised.

I think our reservation here is really unique. We have a lot to offer people. And I don't mean just the Indian people; I mean all the people who come through the reservation. I'm an outsider, and I've never been treated with disrespect. I love this community because they do carry on their traditions, and they're also trying to become self-sufficient. When I see this community being as strong as it is, doing the best they can to get where they're going, I think they'll succeed. We have to have the strengths of both worlds. Before my grandfather passed away, he told me, "We're getting to a time when we're going to have these big computers, machines, and cars everywhere, but never mind all these things; never give up your Indian ways. But you also have to learn how to be white. You'll have to live in both worlds." He left us that to believe.

Dawn Smith

Dawn Smith, a Klamath Indian, has lived on the Warm Springs Reservation and worked there as an educator for twenty-three years. Her husband is a tribal member, as are her two children.

Dawn Smith (AUTHOR PHOTO)

I came here twenty-three years ago, right out of college. I was at the University of Northern Colorado studying deaf education, and the college had a program going with Oregon State. The Confederated Warm Springs Tribes, the School District, and Oregon State University had a partnership recruiting Indian students who were in their final year to come here and intern in the district, and then they were promised they would be hired.

There were six of us who came here and interned in the different schools in the district, and I was hired the next year for first grade. I taught first grade for thirteen years, was a counselor for five years, assistant principal for two, and this is my third year as principal.

I'm the seventh principal since I've been here, so we've been through a lot of school culture changes. Most of the principals who came through were on their way to somewhere else and didn't really have an agenda for here. Hiring was pretty haphazard, and we had a high teacher turnover. We couldn't keep teachers; we were just a stepping-stone out of here for most of them. You know, you came into the district here, and if you minded your p's and q's, you moved on. And I'm talking quite a few years ago, so it's been pretty chaotic a lot of the years I've been here. But as a teacher, you can always go into your classroom and shut the door and do the best you can for your kids, and that's pretty much what a lot of us did.

Right now in the building, we've been able to cut teacher turnover almost to nothing, except for the young parents who keep having babies. We've got a real dedicated staff. For the last few years, when we've hired, we've said, "Don't come if you're not going to stay. If you think you're going to come here so you can go on to somewhere else, you won't get a recommendation. You know, we're trying to turn this school around. It's going to take a long time, and it's going to take hard work, and it's going to take commitment. If you're not willing to do that, I'm telling you right now, don't come. You just won't get a letter of recommendation when you leave."

So now we've got only people who were willing to make a commitment to staying. And in hiring, I look for very high quality people: some teaching skills, yes, but if you hire good people, what I think is that you can help them become really good teachers; whereas, you can hire people that know their subject inside and out, but if they don't understand kids, they aren't effective teachers.

When they made me principal, I asked for a community liaison position in place of an assistant principal, and the school district said yes. Helena Jackson, our community liaison, is invaluable to what we do here—her knowledge of the community, connecting with parents, making connections for us with tribal agencies and departments. She's great.

We're in such a perfect spot right now: a young, highly moti-

Dawn Smith

Warm Springs Elementary School (AUTHOR PHOTO)

vated, deeply caring staff. Of all the people on the staff, I'm one of those who has been here the longest. Our young staff is motivated to learn more: "What else can I do?" "What extra things might work?" We don't have any of the old stuck-in-a-rut, I've-been-doing-it-this-way-for-twenty-years kind of people. Everybody's on a learning curve all the time. They're always asking, "What else can I do?" or "How can I do this better?"

Teaching here has been a challenge. We're only now beginning to figure out things that, intuitively, we knew all along and couldn't quite put a handle on, the kinds of needs the kids have—and that basically comes down to language. The new language program started with kindergarten this year. Right now, in fact, over the holidays, I'm finishing a proposal to the State Department to declare us a bilingual, ESL [English as a Second Language] school.

We want to become a dual-language school, to give the kids proficiency in native languages and in English, because what I've found from my research is pretty much that there's not a competency in either language yet. Ninety-nine percent of the kids here don't speak the Indian languages at all, but they don't speak English *really* either. Yes, they all speak English, but proficiency in English—I hate to say this—is limited. It's as if there was a place in their development where learning the language kind of tapered off, didn't get followed through on, stalled out. From there on, it's kind of been basic communication skills. So we're looking at ways to really enrich the English-learning skills and bring back the native-language skills as well. That's what the dual-language proposal will let us do.

We're going for a Goals 2000 grant on staff development. How do we teach the language? We don't have a clue. We're saying words to kids all the time, but we've learned that they don't really know what we're saying. The Goals 2000 grant would affect the content standards, meeting the benchmarks, things like that, but we can't accomplish that until we have a handle on the language. From everything I know, even when you've got the oral language going, the reading and writing lag far behind where you are with the oral language. Many of our kids don't even score well on an oral language test.

But these teachers do an excellent job. We're on the right path now—behavior problems are at a minimum; everybody knows what they're doing. We go for days without seeing trouble here, and we hold really high expectations in student discipline. If students get sent to my office, it's usually because they made a really silly choice. It's not because they're doing something dangerous or racist. There are intertribal disputes, but I don't know if I would ever call it racism.

We do a lot of teamwork and collaboration with planning. We're always taking the kids farther along, but it's like swimming toward shore with a thousand-pound millstone around your neck. And these teachers are doing it because they're wonderful. They're making progress with the students. But just think—if we figure out more about exactly what we want to accomplish, everything will be much easier.

We need the sheltered English kinds of skills; we need language acquisition and ideas about how language is acquired—and we just don't have that training yet.

And because the teachers here aren't native, their perspective is different from their students'. They don't completely understand what the kids are going through—even the most dedicated ones, and the ones who have been here the longest. They really don't understand.

We always knew kind of what the problem with our students

Dawn Smith

121

was, but we were never able to define it clearly before we started focusing on language. With our charter school—a language program that's like a school within a school—we've started meeting the needs of our students. If we do get our ESL designation, we'll be able to form a partnership with the language school, and that way the charter school will receive additional money.

Now we have Arlene Graham, a Warm Springs native, as a kindergarten teacher. Myra Shawaway, also a native, directs the language program. That program is working well in the kindergarten class here, and there's another native speaker who goes over to the Simnasho classroom and teaches every day. At Simnasho everyone, kindergarten through fourth grade, gets native-language lessons, because there are only twenty students in the whole school. For now, here at Warm Springs Elementary, we have the native-language program only in the kindergarten. Next year, we're moving it into the first grade.

One of the things that I think has been a barrier for the language is that students only have each other to talk to. When students are sitting in classes here, they're not sitting with doctors' kids and lawyers' kids and people who have been to Australia, or with teachers' kids—all kinds of people like that. So they really miss out, because they're always with people who are talking about the same things that they always talk about. There's no real enrichment happening in the classroom that way, and I think it's a big minus.

The bilingual proposal addresses this lack of diversity. It will expand the school year, so we can have more time to cover the curriculum and more time to do extra things. It seems right now that we're going a million miles a minute all the time. We're not just talking about spreading out the days we have, but about adding student contact days, so that we can go out and experience more. We can also bring more into the classroom.

One of the most effective methods for expanding students' experiences that some of our teachers are using now is the story line method. One of the teachers just did a story line unit on a farm. You know—the vet was in with the vet bag, and the EMTs and fire fighters came in when the barn burned down; there was just so much experience happening, and vocabulary, and talking, and discussion, asking questions. Those are the kinds of things we need to have happening more, so we've got to have more time to do them.

We're putting the story line method into our Goals 2000 proposal as part of the partnership. Our story line experiences have strengthened our ties with the Indian Language Program. If the Indian-language teachers could be trained in the method, they could start presenting their curriculum through the story line and actually recreate what the kids have missed out on culturally.

The number of traditional kids in the community is actually not very large, so a lot of the kids have never been introduced to traditions. There may be more kids from Simnasho from traditional homes. It's a little bit more of an intact community. Many of the kids there are in families that have moved back there from this community. I think they're a little bit closer to the longhouse there, and the traditions. A lot of families that have moved back to Simnasho felt close ties to that end of the reservation and to things that were there when they were growing up.

After fourth grade, kids go to the middle school in Madras. When I first came here, the elementary school went through sixth grade. Then, as we grew, we ran out of space. When the new middle school in Madras opened, we moved our fifth and sixth grade there. We're on the road to a new school here, finally. There's been an historic agreement between Jefferson County, the tribes, and the school for a new elementary school. When that happens, I think we'll go back to K through 5.

The transition from the reservation school to Madras is something we're always working on, and I don't think we've nailed it yet. I think in the past there've been a lot of superficial kinds of things that really didn't help much. We can put the kids together more, but it's not really going to make that much of a difference, because when they get over there, they begin being bombarded by the language and the experiences that they haven't had here. So much just goes right over their heads; they feel that they're not really part of what's happening in the classroom. The teachers here are at least aware that there's a comprehension problem, and they try to stay aware of that during the day while they're teaching. Most of the elementary teachers realize that much of what they're saying is not hooking on to what the kids already know.

We can do something about the race relations, which will help kids make the transition to Madras. But the basic information, the teaching that's going on—the students don't really feel a part of it there. I've been talking to the middle-school principal because there's a new administration there, and he *gets* it. He understands the kinds of things that are going to have to happen, so there's hope that the teaching styles will be more the same.

In the past, when our students went to the middle school, the fifth- and sixth-graders were grouped with the seventh- and eighth-graders. It was more of a junior-high philosophy, and that was a disaster. This year, one of the assistant principals is in charge of just the fifth and sixth grades, and they've pulled them back into an elementary-school structure. Our fifth-graders from here are doing better this year.

What we're seeing about the Madras school situation is that putting a thousand kids together in a school creates learning problems for everybody. Here we average twenty kids per class. Class size in Madras goes up to thirty, so it's harder for students to get individual attention. Please don't think I'm saying anything about the school itself—just the structure.

The population of this school has been growing up until this year. This year our kindergarten class dropped, and for the next two years we're expecting the numbers to drop. We were hitting about a hundred kids a grade level for several years, and for the next few years we'll be hitting around seventy-five.

The Warm Springs School District has always afforded us the luxury of small class sizes because they realize we really have to be there for the kids, not just work with them on academics. We have to unlock what's happening inside them, find a way to translate all this wonderful stuff they know into what we're asking for in the public schools. It is a challenge!

Helena Jackson

For four years, Helena Jackson has served as the liaison between the Warm Springs community and their elementary school.

I've lived in Warm Springs all my life, except for four years I spent on the Umatilla Reservation with my first husband. I'm a tribal member, although my dad is Yakama and my mom is Warm Springs, so I'm half Warm Springs myself. I've seen a big change on the reservation since I was a child.

I'm forty years old, and I have three children. Sharon, my oldest, just reached the magic age of twenty-one. I think I was lucky that she saw teenage pregnancy. She worked at Children's Protective Services for our tribe. It was heartbreaking for her to see children that didn't have people to take care of them. One day she came home from work crying and said, "I'm not going to have kids. There's too many kids now who need homes."

It bothers me that our elders are called upon to take care of babies, when the young people having the babies should be taking care of the elders instead.

When I was young, I spent a lot of time with my grandparents on both sides of the family. My dad's mother lived in Rock Creek, Washington, which is a little Indian community outside of Goldendale, Washington. My mom's parents lived in Simnasho. I have a lot of fond memories of my elders, and I learned a lot of important values from them.

After I got out of high school, I made plans to go to business school in Portland, but basically I was one of those people who just wanted to get things over with. Now I'm at an age where I wish I'd gone to a college for at least a year or two.

Helena Jackson (AUTHOR PHOTO)

But Portland didn't work out for me, so I returned home to Warm Springs. After I had my first child when I was nineteen, I started working for the tribe. Since then I've worked in various departments for the tribal organization—fire management, the community center recreation department, tribal management. I've worked in different capacities in the Tribal Council office. I worked as an accountant for the Tribal Council, and as a records manager, and a few times I was called on to fill in as a supervisor, when the supervisors were out of the office. I worked in accounts payable, a very demanding job, before I started what I'm doing now at the grade school.

It used to be that I very seldom read the newspaper, because I didn't have time, but I did see the position I have now advertised—community liaison at Warm Springs Elementary. The job description said a high school diploma was enough, so I decided to send in my résumé, to try it.

Our elementary school is part of the 509-J School District, so I had to go to Madras and fill out my application there. Then I got a call at work from Dawn Smith, the principal. She set up an interview, and it was exciting just getting a chance to be interviewed for the job, because in all the years I'd been working I never thought there might be a job at the elementary school for me.

I went for my interview, and Dawn and I knew each other already, but not in the working world. The first thing she told me was that she was interviewing fourteen people for the position. Right then and there, I thought, "I don't even have a chance." So I'd forgotten all about the interview by the time Dawn called and asked if could come up and talk to her. After we talked for a while, she told me I had the job.

I didn't really know what I was getting myself into with the job of community liaison, because there wasn't a lot of detail in the job description. I ended up pretty much making the job up myself. This has been the best career change I've ever made. Every now and then, I stop and think about how thankful I am to have this job. The other thing I'm thankful for is having such a great boss. Dawn is supportive of me, and she's the first boss I've ever had who says "thank you." At first I was surprised at how much she appreciated the work I was doing.

Back when I went to Warm Springs Elementary myself, we went up to the sixth grade. Then, after the sixth grade, we moved to the junior high at Madras. Now our children go to Madras after the fourth grade. I admire our children for the challenges they face today, because I remember the scary feeling I had leaving grade school in the sixth grade. Even though we went to Madras all the time for bowling and to buy groceries, the thought of going to school over there was really scary. Now I look at our children being

Helena Jackson

bussed to the middle school for fifth grade, and that has to be a lot harder for them.

We have a community liaison in Madras, Foster Kalama, who spends half a day at the high school and half a day at the middle school. We were classmates together. Sometimes I call him, and sometimes he calls me, and we talk about our problems. I admire the job Foster's doing at the middle school, because our children have such a hard time after they leave the grade school here. At one point our people were worried about the kids dropping out of high school, and now they're already dropping out at the middle school. That's too young, entirely too young, to be dropping out of school.

At the elementary school, I don't have to deal with disciplinary problems, which I'm glad about. I try to help Dawn in every other capacity that I'm able to. I attend meetings that she can't get to. I work with outside agencies that want to bring a program to our school.

I helped start the SMART program—Start Making A Reader Today. This is our third year. It's for kindergarten, first, and second grades, and it provides one-on-one help in reading for the children who need it. The biggest challenge is recruiting community members to volunteer their time to come in and read to the kids. The more readers we have, the more children we can get involved. Every year, the program has been more and more successful. Attendance at school is better on SMART days. The first year, we were lucky to get twenty people to come in and read. We probably have close to fifty readers now. This year the Tribal Council donated all the money we needed for the program.

Another part of my job is to work with the tribal organizations on various things: poison prevention, dental hygiene, recycling. I help the secretaries in the school office. I help monitor the computer at the cafeteria. I'm kind of like a public relations person for the school. I'm over at the school cafeteria at seven-thirty every morning, the first one to see the kids when they arrive. I feel bad whenever I see a child coming to school upset or crying, having a bad start to the day. Sometimes I feel like I need to do even more.

I work on attendance with a counselor named Harry Phillips. Kids don't realize that by not coming to school they're getting left behind. That's where I see the frustration starting, when they come back to school and their class has advanced since they left. Harry set up an incentive program for children that have poor attendance, and it's been successful. I've known Harry almost all my life. I remember him playing cards with my dad and his friends, and I remember him as a grade-school teacher. Now I have the honor of working with him his last year. I think he's been here thirty-six or thirty-seven years.

A lot of times we deal with families that don't have a phone, or any friend or relative to deliver a message, so I do it. I go out into the community on home visits if a teacher or a secretary requests it. It might have to do with a child who's been absent, or with a question about a medication. I get signatures when we need them, take children home when they've had an accident or when they're sick.

Simnasho has its own small elementary school, and the kids there also go from kindergarten through fourth grade. I try to link our two schools together, to include Simnasho in as much as possible. They come to Warm Springs for awards assemblies and field trips. We're getting better at not forgetting them, at making them a part of our activities.

Our Honors Seniors Day is coming up in May. Part of my job is to help through the school. It's an annual event conducted by the tribal senior citizens' department, and what we do is host senior citizens from all over, from various reservations, senior centers, and nursing homes. In the past, we've had over six hundred senior citizens here at one time.

A big project that we just finished was for the tribal work experience program. They bought a whole bunch of beads and wanted kids to make necklaces for a national work experience conference in either Reno or Arizona. It sounds easy, but stringing beads is a tough project. We did about 280 necklaces.

There've been a lot of changes since I was in grade school, and computers is one of them. It just amazes me to watch the children here. They want that computer knowledge. They want to be on a computer, and that's neat. I found out working in the tribal offices that a lot of adults are afraid of computers, but the kids can't keep their hands off.

Helena Jackson

We have a year-round school in the beginning stages now. We got a State Department grant to do the planning, and Dawn just recently went on our local radio station, KWSO, and talked about it to educate the community. I'm excited about that.

Sometimes now I work in the summer. For the first couple of years I didn't, and then last year I got a part-time job working with children at the museum, teaching them how to do beadwork. We had eighteen people from the community signed up to teach classes to children at the museum classes—like string work and how to make moccasins. Beadwork helps me make my living. I sell to the two stores down on the plaza, and also at the museum and Kah-Nee-Ta.

Another part of my job is educating the teachers about our community and our culture. I don't claim to know everything, and I always tell them that if I don't know, somebody else in the community will.

There were a number of teachers that started here the same year I did. At the beginning of the school year, they have an orientation for teachers new to the district. At the museum they teach about our culture—what will happen if there's a death in the community, that type of thing. Last year one of the teachers that started with me came up to me—this was during our third year—and said, "When we first started, they talked about death in the community, but back then it didn't mean anything to me. Now that I've been with the kids who are experiencing it and seen how it affects the community and the school, I want to know more." So I always try to get people like that the information they want or need.

This is my fourth year on the job, and I am glad to be a part of everything. It's been a pretty successful four years for me. Every year is a learning experience.

My oldest daughter, who's twenty-one now—I'm really proud of her. Although she doesn't have the college degree, she did go to school in Phoenix, Arizona, and got a lot of training in computers. Right now she's working for the tribe in the Office of Information Systems. She trouble-shoots for departments if they're having troubles with their computers.

She also participated in Futures for the Children in Phoenix, a leadership and training group. She attended a lot of education conferences on the Futures for the Children panel, and I was always proud when people I worked with came up to me and told me, "Oh, I heard your daughter talk at the conference, and she's a real good public speaker." I'm proud of my daughter for the things she's done.

Both my boys have gone to grade school here. Right now they're going to school in Pendleton. My oldest boy's a sophomore this year, and he'll be staying with his dad and grandma in Pendleton until he finishes school.

My first marriage wasn't too successful. My first husband was from the Umatilla tribe. We lasted nineteen years. It's hard on me having my boys so far away.

I just recently remarried. I met a guy, and little did I ever·think that I'd get married a second time. One of the things I learned from my grandparents was that you got married for life. That was instilled in me as a young child. It was really hard for me to divorce my first husband, even if everything was getting so ugly.

I couldn't believe it was really happening to me, and I couldn't make it stop. It was because I really believed that a marriage should last forever, so I stayed with it as long as I could. Finally I started doing other things, like going to community counseling, and I also attended women's support groups. Those things made me feel better about divorcing my first husband.

I just got tired of being the only one trying, so I did file for divorce. It wasn't the end of the world, but I thought it was going to be.

My first husband's family was great to me. In fact, I keep in touch with most of them now, and when my nieces and nephews come to Warm Springs to play softball or basketball or whatever, they make a point of stopping to see me. They still call me "auntie."

I really miss my ex-in-laws too, but now I'm on my second marriage. This is our second year. My husband is from the Klamath tribe, and it's his first marriage. He grew up in the Eagle Point area, a non-Indian community. One of his challenges as an adult now is living in an Indian community. I grew up on the reservation all my life, so sometimes we don't see eye-to-eye on things, but we talk and learn a lot from each other.

Helena Jackson

My youngest child is going to be twelve this year, so I'll have him for a little while longer. Working at the school, I feel I can do a little more for him. I want him to get the education he needs. I encourage him to try harder, get involved with everything he's doing.

I tried to get involved with my two older children, but back in those days, I was working for the tribe and couldn't take the time off to go on field trips. Now, here at the school, I see a lot of parental and community involvement in activities. I don't know if it's because of me, but Dawn told me one time that this involvement has increased since I've been here. I feel glad about that.

From what I understand, they'll build a new elementary school here in Warm Springs. We don't know yet what grade levels will be included. I hope I'm still here when we get the new school.

We see gang activities with our older kids, and then we see little kids mimicking gangs, using gang graffiti. It scares me—they're just copying something, and they don't even realize it's not right.

We pretty much know which of our children are at risk, the ones that are having a hard time at home. Living in the community, working in the community, knowing everybody, confidentiality is a big part of my job. Sometimes you hear from reliable sources what's going on in a family—a child just isn't getting the necessary care, that sort of thing. I don't want to get anybody in trouble, but I do want to make things a little easier for that child.

What it's all about is kids making right choices and wrong choices. One example is my two brothers, who were close in age and given the same opportunities growing up. One of them made the right choices, and the other one made the wrong ones.

That's what it's all about now, teaching kids to make good choices.

I grew up in a family where there wasn't very much hugging. I don't remember my mom or dad telling me that they loved me. I felt it, sensed it, without them having to tell me, but sometimes you need to hear it. Working here at the school, I get hugs every day.

The Deserted Boy

... *[I]f we could just take time from our teaching of our poor
Indians, we might learn something from them.*

        PETER MATTHIESSEN, *At Play in the Fields of the Lord*

Before placing education at the Warm Springs Reservation in the
context of institutionalized Indian education in America, it helps
to recall the kinds of schooling that existed for Indian people for
thousands of years prior to Euro-American contact.

    For the people who formed the Confederated Tribes of Warm
Springs, teaching children and young adults traditionally occurred
as part of everyday life, a process actually far more complex than
the Euro-American model for Indian education. Tribes lived by
the seasonal round, so all healthy adults and adolescents were involved in the necessary work of sustenance and survival. Older
children were enrolled in hands-on learning throughout the year,
while young children enjoyed the company and watchful care of the
elders, those community members who had lived the longest and
presumably knew the most about physical survival, spirituality, the
natural world, cultural traditions, and social negotiations within a
small but complex community. Through games, storytelling, and
personal interaction with youngsters, elders instructed children in
appropriate behavior, tribal history, religion, mythology, and customs associated with hunting, fishing, food gathering and preservation, and various crafts.

    Elders observed children closely and were constantly available
to give instruction at the teachable moment when a youngster,
motivated to accomplish a certain task or desiring to understand
a natural event, requested instruction or asked a question. Though
the primary responsibility for educating the young was borne by

family members, the entire community viewed children as precious natural resources, links to the future to be protected and carefully nurtured. (It is still quite common today to hear Indian people speak of making decisions with the welfare of the seventh generation in mind.)

Children who showed aptitude in certain areas were apprenticed to "specialists," such as a shaman, a storyteller, or a master weaver, carver, potter, or singer. When a child was ready to excel in a particular activity, a tutor was always available. (Without doubt, the pupil-teacher ratio was significantly lower than that found in contemporary American classrooms.)

Personality growth was at the center of traditional Indian education, serving as the foundation for vocation, profession, and daily life. Vine Deloria Jr. makes the point in *Indian Education in America* that this emphasis on personality development marks a major difference between tribal education and modern educational practices. The tension between these philosophies of education emerges in countless conflicts (some subtle, others not so subtle) throughout the history of Indian education in the United States. Margaret Szasz, in the introduction to her landmark study *Education and the American Indian* insists that her historical examination of Indian education between 1928 and 1973 "is the story of the Indian people and their struggles to gain an education that will teach their children not only the fundamentals of mainstream society but also the contributions of their own cultural heritage." Deloria's analysis extends that same concern into the education of Indian children in the 1990s. According to Deloria, "Education today trains professionals but it does not produce people."

Deloria refers to the tendency in Western thought to divide knowledge into categories—to study subjects like geometry as something separate from biology, for example, or writing as separate from literature—and then to distance all of the subjects from real life by insisting on the superiority of objectivity. This notion of knowledge as a refined, concise product separated from personality growth can cause insurmountable problems for Indian students from traditional backgrounds, because in Indian tradition, no such separation exists.

Children with tribal connections are apt to see the world in terms of relationships: people have knowledge of certain natural events or phenomena, for instance, because of a relationship that existed with the long-ago people and their animal helpers/teachers. Deloria explains that "traditional knowledge enables us to see our place and our responsibility within the movement of history. Formal American education, on the other hand, helps us to understand how things work, and knowing how things work and being able to make them work, is the mark of a professional person in this society. . . . [F]or many Americans there is no personal sense of knowing who they are, so professionalism always overrules the concern for persons." The educational issues raised by Wilson Wewa Jr., Dawn Smith, Helena Jackson, Foster Kalama, and others interviewed here reflect these same concerns at the Warm Springs Reservation.

Looking back at the form and function of the educational experiences provided for American Indians—quite often forced upon them by the government—we can only conclude that, until recently, American Indian education was designed to destroy the personality, self-esteem, and cultural identity of the individual child in the name of assimilation into the mainstream culture. Beginning officially with a mandate from the Continental Congress in 1776 to contract teachers for New York Indians, the federal government's intention to use education as a tool in territorial expansion was clear.

Jorge Noriega, in his extensively documented essay "American Indian Education in the United States: Indoctrination for Subordination to Colonialism" (in *The State of Native America*, edited by M. Annette Jaimes), details the development of a U.S. model for Indian education. Throughout the nineteenth century, the government put aside the notion of separation of church and state and relied primarily on missionaries from the Presbyterian and Dutch Reform churches, and later the Methodist Episcopal Society, to deliver an Indian education program. Mission schools instructed students in letters, manual labor, mechanical arts, morals, and Christianity. Children were forbidden to speak their native languages, practice their religions, or wear traditional clothing. The school/work day began at four o'clock in the morning and ended at eight o'clock at night.

As the number of mission schools grew, a system of manual labor schools—the first of which was the Choctaw Academy, founded in 1834 in Scott County, Kentucky—was begun. Noriega calls these schools an experiment in modified slavery that included forced labor for crop production. Many of the costs related to keeping Indian children at the mission schools, labor schools, or boarding schools were offset by the institutional labor performed by the children themselves.

Though day schools were less expensive to operate, the government favored boarding schools because children could be more effectively shielded from the "contaminating" cultural influences of home and family. At the Carlisle Indian School in Carlisle, Pennsylvania (their most famous pupil was Sac Indian Jim Thorpe, often called the best male athlete in the history of America), students were not allowed to return home during the summer for vacations. Instead, they were hired out for labor and had their wages confiscated by school officials.

Along with the military assaults launched against the Indian people in the name of manifest destiny, the government's educational campaign to annihilate native cultures rivals the treatment of black slaves in the American South as a demonstration of codified racism and brutality. The government worked diligently to separate young Indians from their roots, to Americanize them by erasing who they were and supplanting that identity with a personality groomed for subservience in the dominant culture. Voluminous evidence of this is found in annual reports to Congress from federal Indian agents, in reports produced by officials of the mission and boarding schools, and in accounts of boarding school experiences recorded in the diaries of Indian people who were subjected to this treatment. Foster Kalama of Warm Springs blames the anger and hostility that he has witnessed from his mother and her generation on the physical, sexual, verbal, and emotional abuse that these people suffered as children in the boarding schools (see interview).

Children whose very identities were systematically besieged by a powerful institutional force, as in the boarding schools, had few psychological defenses; but at least children belonging to long-house societies, like those of the Warm Springs tribes, had been exposed to survival stories and stories of young people discovering inner strengths in the face of adversity.

A Wasco tale, "A Deserted Boy is Protected by Itch'əxian's Daughter," recorded by Jeremiah Curtain at the Warm Springs Reservation in 1885, addresses issues of knowledge, identity, and appropriate behavior. Though the story alerts young people to the value of knowing traditional ways and the importance of discovering one's special role in a community, it also provides a metaphorical framework for thinking about the Warm Springs people and their experience with and responses to an educational system imposed upon them by an alien society.

According to Curtain's 1885 version of the story, the chief of a village decides to move his people to another location, deliberately abandoning a young boy who is strong but quarrelsome. The child's grandmothers leave him some fire in a shell, a deer rib with which to make fish hooks, and ten wild potatoes.

The boy experiences loneliness and sometimes even cries, but he never despairs. Using the gifts from his grandmothers (traditional knowledge and tools), he feeds and clothes himself. As the story unfolds, it becomes clear that the boy, rather than being "bad," is an exceptional person. Possibly the chief feared him because he had shown early signs of leadership, superiority, and power.

An important instructional element of this story, aimed at young audiences, is that the child never once questions his own self-worth, not even when he is rejected by the group. He has confidence in his native skills and relies on his knowledge of traditional ways. The story's ending indirectly illustrates the responsibility of each successive generation to move forward and adapt to life's changes while maintaining the values of preceding generations.

In a mythic time frame, the boy grows to manhood in five days. He sings a song by the river and is rewarded with material gifts of food and shelter from the daughter of the water chief Itch'əxian. The mystical daughter becomes his wife, and when the people of the village discover the young man's success, they ask to return to their original site and enjoy the abundance of fish received by the

The road to Simnasho (AUTHOR PHOTO)

river chief's daughter each day. The young man willingly shares his wealth and welcomes the villagers back, except for the chief, whom he drowns in the river by causing a storm to rise.

This myth tells as much about the community's failure to appreciate the potential blessings that an exceptional child might bestow on the group as it does about the child's accomplishments. The community, influenced by a jealous chief, abandons a child who has the potential to bring wealth to everyone. Metaphorically, we might easily relate the misguided villagers to the people of power in America's dominant society, and the child might represent the Indian nations—in this specific context, the people of Warm Springs.

The United States government confiscated vast tracts of Indian lands, assumed power over the indigenous peoples of these lands, and abandoned them on reservations. The "chief" (i.e., the federal government) not only ignored the special knowledge and talents of Indian people; it sought to destroy that knowledge in Indian children. The ultimate goal of institutionalized Indian education was, clearly and simply, the obliteration of indigenous cultures.

Of course, the longhouse storyteller, as he performed the tale of the deserted boy, had nothing resembling this late-twentieth-century "reading" in mind; nevertheless, the values gleaned by those who heard the story have surely played a part in the survival of the Warm Springs people and their culture against great odds.

It is also worth noting the evolution of the story itself from the 1885 recording by Curtain to a 1919 version collected by Edward Sapir in *Wishram Texts* (New York: American Ethnological Society, 1974). When Louis Simpson told the story of the deserted boy to Sapir a few decades after an anonymous storyteller had related it to Curtain, one important detail had been altered: at the end of the story, the boy destroys not just the chief, but all of the villagers as well, except for the grandmothers. The abandoned child has become skeptical and vindictive. Though confident in his own strength, he is only willing to trust and to save the relatives who had given him the knowledge and tools that kept him alive until he made his own connections in the world.

By the time of the 1855 treaty with the Confederated Tribes of Warm Springs, which required that the United States provide educational services to the tribes, the federal government had already established an assimilationist, or colonialist, model for Indian education. Tribal leaders, though, certainly did not intend to cease educating young people in as many traditional ways as could be maintained while living on a restricted land base; and they also hoped to better prepare their children for a future that would include participation in the white culture that now surrounded them.

The treaty promised the people of Warm Springs one schoolhouse and one schoolteacher. Children were to continue living with their families, learning community values and gaining traditional knowledge, while also accumulating skills at school needed for a new way of life. But when the first schoolhouse at the Agency didn't open until seven years after the signing of the treaty, and the building that did open was so poorly constructed that it couldn't be used during cold weather (the very season, traditionally, when young people wouldn't be needed for food gathering), it must have been difficult — if not impossible — for tribal members to generate respect for formal education.

A boarding school, completed in the early 1870s, lacked sufficient space and supplies. A makeshift school was built in Simnasho in 1874, and in 1880 the government established an off-reservation boarding school for Indians of the Northwest tribes in Forest Grove, Oregon, more than one hundred miles across the Cascade Mountains from Warm Springs. Fifteen children from the Warm Springs Reservation were in its first class. This school was later moved to Salem and became Chemawa Indian School. Thus, twenty-five years after the original treaty agreement, children from Warm Springs fell victim to an educational system that not only physically separated them from family and community, but sought to destroy their intellectual, emotional, and psychological connections to tribal identity as well.

By the time dormitories and classrooms for compulsory boarding school were constructed at the Warm Springs Agency in 1897, many families refused to send their children to school. A century later, irregular attendance of the Warm Springs children enrolled in Warm Springs Elementary and the Madras middle and high schools remains a problem. Foster Kalama, the Warm Springs community liaison with the Madras school district, reports that of 300 Warm Springs children enrolled at Madras Middle School in 1996–1997, 125 of them were absent each day.

Attendance statistics such as those cited above clearly indicate that phasing out the boarding school system and placing Indian children in public schools hasn't satisfied the educational needs of Indians in America. This failure isn't surprising, given the origin of the campaign to place Indians in public schools and the documented mishandling of both federal money and curriculum issues that has been associated with the movement from the beginning.

In the 1920s, various constituents in the U.S. Congress began seeking ways to accelerate the assimilation of natives into mainstream culture and to rid the government of the costly business of administering Indian affairs. Coercing Indian children to attend public schools was at the heart of this campaign. The Snyder Act of 1921 authorized the Bureau of Indian Affairs to establish and fund educational programs to benefit Indians and to subsidize public schools that enrolled Indian students. To answer complaints that the Indians were not citizens of the United States, that tribal lands could not be taxed, and that education of Indians was a federal responsibility, Congress passed the Indian Citizenship Act in 1924.

Dolores Huff, in *To Live Heroically: Institutional Racism and American Indian Education*, explains that government efforts to move toward placing more Indian children in public schools were aided by an attack on the BIA by a group of reputable intellectuals and philanthropists known as the Committee of One Hundred. Claims of BIA misconduct led to a 1928 congressional investigation and an extremely negative report entitled "Survey of the conditions of the Indians of the United States."

Shortly thereafter, the Meriam Report, commissioned by Secretary of the Interior Hubert Work and carried out by the Brookings Institution, offered an even more scathing review of BIA mishandling of Indian education. Dr. W. Carson Ryan of Swarthmore College conducted the education segment of the Meriam Report and detailed the inhumane treatment of children in the boarding schools, finding that they were underfed, overworked, and undereducated. Ryan proposed the development of a cross-cultural curriculum in the boarding schools, the establishment of more day schools for Indian children, and, ultimately, increased enrollment of Indian children in public schools. But even when reform-minded people such as Ryan spoke out for what they believed was best for Indian education, Indian people themselves were rarely consulted in the planning.

Capitalizing on Ryan's recommendations, Congress passed a law referred to as the Act of February 15, 1929, authorizing state officials to enter Indian-occupied lands and force Indian children who were not under government supervision to attend public schools in accordance with state laws. (The lawmakers were quite likely more

interested in reducing federal dollars in Indian subsidies than in improving Indian education.)

In spite of these efforts, the federal government, to this day, has not been able to withdraw specific support of Indian education. John Collier, who became Commissioner for Indian Affairs in 1933, was able to get the Indian Reorganization Act and the Johnson O'Malley Act through Congress in 1934. The Indian Reorganization Act promised vocational education for Indians, while the Johnson O'Malley Act (JOM) authorized contractual agreement with states to pay for the education of Indian children in the public school system. Even after the Warm Springs Constitution established its own Tribal Council and government, the U.S. government still held trust obligations that included provisions for health and education.

In 1975 the Indian Self-Determination and Education Assistance Act allowed for tribal government control over education. Guy Senese, in his book-length study *Self-Determination and the Social Education of Native Americans,* analyzes how the meaning of "Indian control" evolved over the decades between JOM and the Indian Self-Determination Act. The O'Malley Act designated dollars to support Indian children in public schools; but the BIA, not the Indians themselves, controlled those dollars. Placing the BIA in charge of funds to improve public education for Indians and reduce the need for BIA schools produced an obvious contradiction within the agency itself. If public school programs and Indian community-controlled contract schools actually resulted in better education for native children, the BIA, an agency that has always worked hardest to maintain its own existence, would lose control of a major segment of its operations.

To complicate matters further, America's involvement in World War II and postwar reorganization policies shifted Indian education efforts away from cross-cultural curriculum and native language programs back to the development of work habits and training for industrial jobs. Government efforts to take control of natural resources on Indian lands cannot be separated from the education efforts to distance native children from their cultural roots, to move Indians off the reservations, and to push them once again toward assimilation. Indian people should have been trained to manage their own natural resources; but timber, oil, and minerals were in demand by American industry, so instead, Indians were trained to provide the manual labor to support industry.

As the official assimilation efforts of the 1940s and 1950s continued, resistance among white reformers and Indian leadership groups strengthened. In 1944 the National Congress of American Indians was organized. In 1961 the Udall Task Force and the Fund for the Republic Commission on the Rights, Liberties and Responsibilities of the American Indians brought native educational issues to national attention once again.

After the 1968 report of the Senate Select Subcommittee on Indian Education (headed by Robert Kennedy) confirmed that recommendations made in the Meriam Report had never been fulfilled, the Office of Economic Opportunity (OEO) began a variety of Head Start programs for Indian preschoolers. When OEO funds targeted for Indian-controlled schools, along with dollars from JOM, represented more than half of the BIA operating budget, the agency could no longer ignore the voices of Indian leaders who wanted to be involved in educational policy-making.

In *To Live Heroically*, Huff reports that initially the BIA monitored the use of JOM funds targeted for services to Indian children in the public schools. But school districts balked at the interference of an outside agency, and eventually no one monitored use of the money. In 1971, the NAACP Legal Defense and Educational Funds and the Center for Law and Education at Harvard University conducted a study on the effects of public education on Indian children. The published report, *An Even Chance* (Cambridge: Harvard University Press, 1971), included an evaluation of the Jefferson County schools in Madras, Oregon, where it found that Indian children were charged for their lunches and had to pay in advance, even though JOM provided for school lunches. The report further noted that in school districts all over the country, Indian children were being stigmatized for accepting the free lunches for which, in Madras and probably in other places, they were actually paying. Furthermore, dollars designated for special projects to meet the needs of Indian children were used to benefit all children, thus circumventing the intent of the law. Although federal dollars were earmarked for specific curricular efforts, and although Indian communities wanted tribal history, language, and culture in the curriculum, school officials refused to recognize these subjects as legitimate academic concerns.

At the conclusion of his discussion of postwar Indian education policy, Guy Senese succinctly describes the undercurrents of community control and school reform that led to contract schooling:

> *Indian educational self-determination grew out of the efforts of a variety of reform-minded forces and as a result, there was a tacit return to Indian education policy which emphasized cross-cultural and community-controlled education. Unfortunately, as the dreams of Indian nationalists and reformers were forged into policy, much of the meaning of the notion of Indian control changed. Indian control, for self-determination and the impulse it represented, was never intended by its key architects to confer to Indian people any legitimate degree of control over their own destiny. Nor were cross-cultural curricula designed primarily as part of an admission that Indian language and culture studies were an end in themselves. Rather, these efforts and the community contract school which represented them were, very much like their counterpart efforts in reservation economic development, a part of a sophisticated economic development model designed to give the appearance of competency to an Indian community.*

To Indians, Indian-controlled education meant cultural and political sovereignty. Self-determination promised a way of holding on to traditional culture, of preserving what was left and recovering, where possible, what had been lost. To the federal government, self-determination as it developed in the wake of the Johnson administration's War on Poverty was viewed as a way out of the financial trust responsibilities of the treaties. If Indians could advance economically and socially, went the reasoning of the government's Indian bureaucracy, they could assimilate more rapidly. Federal thinking on the matter boiled down to this: "Let the Indians help us figure out how to make them more like us."

The February 26, 1998, edition of *Spilyay Tymoo* contains excerpts from statements made by tribal members in meetings or in annual reports of past decades. Here is a comment by Ralph Minnick from the 1983 annual report:

> Tribal government continues to grow and evolve while protecting the source of its creation, the Treaty. Wise leadership, foresight on the part of the elders and continual vigilance by the membership has brought Warm Springs from federal dependency to a successful self-governing reservation within fifty years.

The "continual vigilance" referred to by Mr. Minnick certainly characterizes the reservation's attention to education in recent years. Just as the people of Warm Springs have progressed steadily toward economic autonomy by taking charge of their timber industry, working against very steep odds to develop a fisheries management plan, and building the Kah-Nee-Ta resort, now they are taking charge of the curriculum and teacher training for the elementary education program. More tribal members are getting involved in the daily operation of the middle school and high school in Madras, and the native languages program for the entire community is a high priority of the Culture and Heritage Committee.

Tribal concerns have become a priority at Warm Springs Elementary (WSE), where teachers receive cultural training during the summers and the principal is designing a year-round school. Hoping to reduce middle-school and high-school dropout rates by increasing literacy and self-esteem in their elementary-age children, educators at WSE have created a bookstore where every book costs one dollar. Organized by Wanda Buslach in 1995, the reading assistance program (SMART — Start Making A Reader Today) features fifty community volunteers who give children one-on-one assistance in reading on a weekly basis. *Spilyay Tymoo* profiles SMART volunteers once a month to encourage more members of the community to volunteer.

To engage children in authentic writing tasks, WSE created a "school mail" post office project. Classrooms invented street and city names that were combined into a school mail directory, giving each child an address. Pupils write to one another and to their teachers, counselors, and principal. Children also publish their work in the *Spilyay Tymoo*. A special edition featuring photos and stories by second-graders appeared in February 1998.

In recent years, from the Mohawk country of the east coast to the Hawaiian Islands, there has been a powerful movement toward self-identity through the restoration of native languages. There are currently thought to be only four Wasco speakers, three Northern Paiute speakers, and twenty-five to fifty Sahaptin speakers at Warm Springs. As WSE principal Dawn Smith points out in her interview, educational leaders on the Warm Springs Reservation have concluded that a strong native language program will help elementary pupils in all subject areas, as well as in social skills.

Dawn is working to procure State Department funding to make WSE a dual-language school, where children may become proficient in native languages and in English simultaneously. Lessons given in Wasco, Paiute, and Sahaptin at the elementary school are printed in *Spilyay Tymoo* and broadcast on the tribal radio station, KWSO, to encourage adult involvement.

Myra Shawaway, the language program coordinator, explains the emphasis on language education at Warm Springs: "I guess what we're trying to do is instill some self-identity I think we've lost through the many, many years of becoming part of the mainstream. . . . We think it's real important that our languages not be lost. There's a real depth and feeling. Some of our real feeling words—there are no words in English for them." (On a recent morning when native language study was the topic on a KWSO talk show, a woman called in to tell how her grandfather had explained to her that no word for "giving something back to the earth" existed in English. "Sacrifice" came closest, but it wasn't correct, because giving something back was more obligation than sacrifice; but "obligation" wasn't quite right either, because it implied coercion. They concluded that English was a left-brain language, good for technical matters but often inadequate for references to nature.)

In many ways, the educational reforms currently under way at Warm Springs reflect a return to traditional tribal education as practiced before Euro-Americans put themselves in charge of the process. Children are indeed learning their native languages. Increasing numbers of caring adults are volunteering their time to nurture the young learners. The museum at Warm Springs sponsors classes in traditional crafts such as beadwork and root bag weaving. In spite of the seductive distractions of modern video games and mindless television programming, the educational leaders at Warm Springs are having some success in engaging young people in the study of traditional languages and crafts.

Just as important as the emphasis on early childhood education is the support for adolescents in the public schools in Madras. The children who must travel to Madras to attend school now have access to a tribal counselor who mediates quarrels before they erupt in violent encounters, and who teaches youngsters to take responsibility for their actions and reminds them of their responsibility to their elders and to their future children. Like the deserted boy in the old Wasco tale, the youngsters who leave the reservation to enter school in Madras may feel abandoned at first; but if they learn to believe in themselves and find the help they need, they will probably survive; they may, in fact, prosper.

Foster Kalama

Foster Kalama serves as the liaison between Warm Springs and the public schools in Madras.

Foster Kalama (AUTHOR PHOTO)

When I grew up on this reservation, it was a real rough time. I grew up in an alcohol environment. I was just about a mile and a half, two miles up the creek from the community here. My grandfather was part Hawaiian and part Wasco. My great-great-grandfather was named John Kalama. His parents were King Kamehameha and Queen Kalama. He came into Kalama, Washington, when he was sixteen, seventeen years old, and they named the town after him. He had a son named Peter Kalama who is the father of my grandfather, Henry Kalama, my dad's father. Henry and Rose Kalama lived up the creek. She was from a chief's family. My mom's family was Klickitat and Nez Percé. Chief Joseph's daughter was my mom's dad's mother.

My mother never drank. We worked together out in the fields—raspberry and strawberry fields, blackberries, cherry orchards. We also worked out in the potato fields. I helped my mom provide for our family, growing up. When my dad was home, he was a logging truck driver. My dad was a great provider when he was home, but alcohol tore him away from our home a lot.

I had four sisters. One got hit and killed by a drunk driver. I have five brothers, and I'm the second to the oldest. I have a half-brother from my dad who got shot, probably back around 1980. His name was Norman. My mother had another son, older than me, whose name was Melvin. We had a big family.

When my mother got a real nice job finally, she left me at home, fending for my brothers and sisters a lot, trying to keep them safe while my mother was at work. We had a lot of good neighbors, which was good for us; but it was pretty rough at times, because older boys from other families picked on us quite a lot. I kept my brothers and sisters safe by taking them to certain places where nobody could bother us.

We moved from home to home until we finally ended up in the West Hills area when I was about twelve years old. I lived practically my whole life on the reservation, until I got to be a young adult. There was a lot of family feuding, a lot of jealousy, a lot of hatred around here. I think a lot of that was because of the boarding schools.

My mother went to boarding school. Our people were mistreated there. I heard a lot of stories about it. Here on the Warm Springs Reservation, the boys and girls both were mistreated badly at the Agency school. I understand that at a lot of boarding schools our people were abused physically, sexually, verbally, and emotionally. I think this is where the anger came from in our community, especially with the older people, from my age on up. I'm forty-two years old, and I've seen the anger since I was a little kid.

All my family, including my dad, they all died from alcoholism, cirrhosis, suicide. There was one that was murdered. My dad, he drank and passed out under a picnic table because he couldn't find a place to sleep. This was over in Wasco, Washington, with a foot of snow on the ground. He ended up with double pneumonia and went into one coma after another. He lived five years after that, and I was really grateful, because he came to know the Lord. He asked me to forgive him. One time I was told that the Caucasian people killed their god and put him up on a cross. I believed that, but today I know that Jesus died for all of us. I'm a Christian now.

My dad was there for me all my life, off and on, and he gave me a lot of good things. The thing that hurt the most was that he wasn't there when he was drinking. He was gone anywhere from three months to a year at a time, so I didn't get to know my dad that well as a kid growing up. But he taught me to be a gentleman, and he had a sense of humor. He never hit me.

I became a Columbia River Treaty fisherman at the age of nine years old. I fished on the Columbia twenty-seven fall seasons, and lots of winter, spring, and summer seasons, too. Then they cut us off, and now it's basically winter and fall seasons that we can fish. But I haven't fished in the last two years because of the way the salmon have been depleted.

I learned how to catch fish every possible way when I was growing up. I remember when my dad and I went and gaffed fish up along the Warm Springs River. I was only eight years old when we were gaffing salmon. I used to snag; I used to trap; I used to gill-net; I dipnetted, set-netted on scaffolds. I drifted with gill nets, did all that kind of fishing. I did a lot of my living on the river.

I also hunted since the age of eight. I was already out there walking in the woods with my dad, and he would send me on a drive when we hunted together. I'd circle around, he'd circle around, and I'd chase the deer to him.

I've also worked out in the woods planting trees, and as a woodcutter. I've thinned trees. I did a lot out there in the woods for seven or eight seasons. In the mill I was a veneer puller on the green chain, and I was a chain boss. I was a jitney driver, a clipper man, a bander man, and a stacker man. I did all those jobs, but then one day I started getting sick. I blamed it on something coming off the wood that was affecting me. Something made my spleen and liver swell, and the doctors told me I had to find another job.

So I started volunteering a lot of my time. I put on thirty-some basketball tournaments for youth from ten to eighteen years old. Every one of my tournaments had something to do with education. One time I called my team the Bears. It was out of a 4-H program I joined. The BEARS stood for Better Education Always Receives Satisfaction. We always gave little speeches about unity and how we needed to start working harder toward building our community and forming better relationships with one another. It went well, and one time I had more than sixty girls playing in different age groups. We traveled all over the state playing tournaments, and one year we won thirty straight tournaments.

I also took a lot of kids hiking out in the wilderness, up into the mountain areas, all over the place. I was a victim assistance volunteer. I got called one day by the victim assistance to ask if I'd be willing to be a children's advocate. I told them I'd give it a try, and they trained me real well, and I was a children's advocate for a year.

That job ran out after a year, and then I qualified to be a tribal juvenile probation officer. In that job, I was doing juveniles all the way up to adults sixty-six years old. At one time I had seventy clients under me. Once, when my supervisor and another officer went off to train for a month, I ran the whole office.

Then I turned around and got sick again. I laid myself off and had my supervisor fill my position in, because there was so much work there. I thought I'd better move on and let somebody take that spot.

At first I thought I'd made a mistake, but then here came a tribal prosecutor's position. I have a little court experience, and I went into a program as a paralegal worker. Over a three-year period in the prosecutor's office, I must have had over a thousand hours of on-the-job training.

Then the liaison job came open, and it was something I'd always wanted to do, to work with youth. I don't know how many people applied for it, but several did, and most of them were pretty well qualified for the job. But I was the one who ended up with it.

Foster Kalama

When I first started there, I asked my supervisor what he saw me doing at the school, and he told me I'd have to be a man with many hats. I knew I was the person in between the community and the schools, but where was I supposed to start?

There are seven hundred Native American youth in the middle school and the high school in Madras. I work with them and their parents, and with the departments down here in Warm Springs. Sometimes I meet with the Tribal Council and the education board. I also work with the attendance officer, and all the teachers and the principals, and the other counselors—but most of all I work with the youth. I've tried to work with parents too, to invite them up to the school, but it's been really, really hard to get parent involvement.

I work with gangs, trying to get them to change their ways. They mainly want to be in gangs because they see movies and they see other gangs, and they think that's what they want. They want to be noticed, so they cause trouble to get attention. They dress like gang members; they act like gang members; they do anything to get themselves in trouble. This activity is even going on down as far as the elementary level.

I'll tell you right now that the peer pressures are really bad. I think the problem is 70, 75 percent peer pressure. The other 25 or 30 percent are coming out of alcohol and drug environments. There's always a handful of kids having troubles at home because of alcohol and drugs.

I basically tell our kids that I'm tired of seeing our Native American people being nothing but statistics—the highest alcohol rate, the highest drop-out rate. I tell them they're our future. I ask them if I'm going to be safe when I'm their elder, if their kids are going to be safe when they come to this school. It's up to them how our lives are going to be, our futures.

I work with kids that are hurting real bad. Some of them threaten suicide, and there's sexual abuse. There are a lot of the same things I've gone through. To help deal with it, I made a chart that I call my flow chart. It's worked a lot of wonders with a lot of kids. I haven't had to use it for a long time because I ran through it with every kid. It's a huge cycle of education and life. Education is at the top, and down at the bottom it's got release on it—releasing your hurts, past and present. Off to the right it's got a box I call the garbage box, which has "dead-end" and "powerless" on it. In the garbage box you've got denial, and then it drops down to guilt and shame, court, jail, neglect, rejection. I've had so many tears in my office. If they all stayed there I think they'd fill up the office.

After I'd been working with the Native American kids, the Hispanic kids started coming to see me. Caucasian kids come to see me, too. One day a kid peeked around the corner and asked me, "Are you Foster Kalama?" I told him I was, and he said, "Are you just here for the Indian people?" I said, "You're not talking to me, are you?" So he asked me again, "Are you just for the Indian kids?" So I told him, "You're looking at a person that's color-blind here."

I work with anybody who wants help. So this Caucasian kid walked in and sat down, and I found out he'd been having a lot of problems with several Native American boys. It turned out to be twelve boys, so I got them all in my office and sat them down and basically put them in this Caucasian kid's shoes. I asked them how they'd feel if they were alone with a bunch of people against them. At the end, they turned out to be friends.

I do a lot of mediation. Anything to do with the youth, I work as hard as I can. Parents call me constantly to ask me to help out with their kids, and I do my best. They call me at two, three, four in the morning and ask me who their daughter hangs around with, because the daughter, a seventh- or eighth-grader, isn't home yet. Sometimes I can help, and they find their kid. Once in a while they'll thank me. I don't get a lot of thanks for the things I do, but that's all right; it doesn't bother me. As long as I can help a kid, it doesn't matter.

Besides working as a liaison, I still help out with the prosecutor's office. I'm on a victim impact panel, and I talk to groups. The largest group I ever talked to here on the reservation was about thirty drunken drivers. I'm stern about the ways we need to change. I talk about how right now, as I'm speaking, there's a kid out there being sexually abused. There are several kids out there being physically abused because their parents are drinking. It's over our heads, and we need to start doing things about it. We have to work toward bettering our community.

I've also been involved with several conferences. The first one was a sexual abuse conference, which I spoke at. I spoke about myself being sexually abused as a kid, when I was ten years old. And my older brother, Larson Kalama—he's my first cousin, but we call each other brother—helped set up a healing of veterans and families conference. This year it was here, and after it's been to Montana and Texas, it will circle back this way, and on the seventh year it's going to be right here again. My brother does the healing circle, and he also works in the sweat lodge.

He invites me up by Tacoma, Washington, to help with the veterans there. We drum and sing in the sweat lodge and do a lot of prayers. My brother does the healing circle. I talk to kids up there. The last time my brother called me up there, it was all Caucasian kids and one colored guy. They were all smart, athletic kids, some even from doctors' families.

I coach here in the middle school, seventh- and eighth-grade girls. This year I coach the intra-murals, the girls who didn't make the traveling team. Last year I coached the traveling team. At Warm Springs, practically everybody loves basketball or softball, and we have some volleyball. We've got some pretty strong teams here on the reservation. They really work hard.

In a way, I have a kind of thankless job. No matter what you do, there's a lot of jealousy and anger and hate. One of the things I notice about our tribe is that we have longhouse against longhouse, family against family. Some of the most prejudiced people I've ever met in my life are right here on the reservation.

As a kid growing up, I ran into prejudice from other races, mainly the Caucasian race. I've had beer bottles and rocks thrown at me. I've had garbage thrown at me. When I boxed—I fought for eight years—I was called "dirty Indian" and "wagon burner."

I went to Indian school in '73, '74, and '75. I started a boxing club there. When I first got there, there were a lot of fights. Pretty soon it was down to almost no fights at all, except girls fighting with each other. All the boys quit fighting because the boxing had settled everybody down.

Before I started working at the high school, I heard there used to be three to five fights every week. It's dropped down to very few fights every year now. This is my third year there, and—don't take

Madras Mid-High (AUTHOR PHOTO)

it wrong, but the last fight there was between a Caucasian and a Hispanic. I was glad it wasn't an Indian, but there shouldn't be any fights at all. The fights that do surface are usually because the kids are having a rough time at home. Last year we only had nine fights, and this year there haven't been many yet.

At the middle school it's pretty rough. The first year I started there, the kids were very hateful and angry. I'd be walking down the hall, and they'd be glaring at me and asking me what the blankety-blank I was doing there, what the blankety-blank I was looking at. I heard the worst, until I started bringing them into my office in little groups and basically telling them, "Hey, I know your grandparents; I know your parents; I know your brothers and sisters. I know everybody in Warm Springs Reservation." After a while, they settled down.

One thing the kids don't do anymore when we talk, like they did when I first got there, is blame anything on teachers or principals. It all comes down to peer pressure, home environment, and alcohol and drugs. I hear very little about teachers anymore.

But I see a lot of frustrated teachers, because a lot of the kids are out of control. They walk out of class anytime they feel like it. They use the worst language you can imagine. When I walk down the hall and say hello to teachers and ask how their day's going, sometimes they walk right on by me like I don't even exist. When

Foster Kalama

I can, I try to tell the teachers that the kids are going to treat us the way we treat them. If we look at the kids from terrible environments sideways, they'll feel the rejection, and then they'll be disruptive.

I used to do a lot of home visits. This year I spend more of my time working with the kids, because the home visits don't usually help much. I turn around and leave, and they shut the door on me and drink some more.

So I work with the youth. I tell them that they have a future. Nobody owns their future; not even us parents own their futures. We're there to provide for them. I tell them that if it's bad at home, it's up to them to break the cycle of alcohol and drugs.

This is my twelfth year of sobriety. I used to be an alcoholic. I was a drug addict. I was sexually abused at the age of ten by an old neighbor man. I've shared this story but never use names, and I don't want to hurt anybody, even though I was hurt at the time.

I was asked to be a keynote speaker at a conference in San Diego. To my surprise, Janet Reno was another speaker there. If I can serve my people, or serve any people, I'm strong enough to be willing to talk about being sexually abused. If I can find release in my heart from these things, I'm only going to feel better.

I've been through a lot of things. I grew up with my grandparents until I was six or seven years old, and then I went back to my parents. For a time I felt like we were complete strangers.

I used to be abducted by my aunts when they wanted a car to take off in. They'd tell my grandmother they were going to the store for something, and I'd be in the car, and we'd end up in Portland. I'd be in the back of the car, cold and hungry, while my aunts were inside the tavern drinking. Sometimes I'd be out there from opening time all the way up to closing time.

So I've lived a pretty ugly life at times. But the best times I've had were along the creek and along the Deschutes River, hunting and hiking in the hills all over the reservation. I know the whole reservation inside and out. I've done a lot of rafting and boating, especially on the Columbia River.

I feel like I've accomplished a lot. I think if, when I was in school, there'd been somebody to go to, like the kids can come to me, it would have helped a lot. I never had anybody to go to. The only time I ever went up to the front office was when I got called up there and got paddled. Back then we got paddled for anything—chewing gum, even whispering to our neighbor across the aisle or passing on a note.

I went to Madras High School until I was a sophomore, and then I went to Indian school. I was three credits short when I dropped out and started into the alcohol world. Then I got my GED later on.

In the alcohol world I fought a lot with guys from gangs. I'd fight with the toughest guy and beat him up. I lived over on the Yakima Indian Reservation for a few years, and all I ever did was fight and play pool and fish on the Columbia. I'd go back and forth, back and forth between fishing and the reservation.

For years I drank my life away. I've been through a lot of car wrecks. I've been shot at several times—once in Tacoma, once in Portland, once in Salem, once here in Warm Springs. I've had knives pulled on me several times. I've been hit with chains, pool sticks, pool balls, wine bottles, beer bottles, rocks, clubs. You name it, I've been hit with it. I've been kicked with probably every boot in the book. I guess I have a hard Hawaiian head.

I've seen a lot of death in my life due to alcoholism. I've lost friends to drowning because they were hung over and got cramps and couldn't make it back to shore. I had a friend who just came out from a big drunk and tried to go in the sweat lodge and landed right on top of the rocks with his head and burned to death. I've lost several family members through car accidents. One of my best friends I lost was up in Alaska. He went out on the river to run some gill nets, and when he fell in, he didn't last more than ten seconds. He froze to death right there in the water. His name was Joe Hawk.

I talk to the kids very strong, and I'm positive with them. I give them positive strokes whenever I can. I let them know that whenever I get a chance, I brag about them. I think that helps them with their esteem. I use my life, the way I was, to relate to what they're going through. I'm seeing a lot of these kids turning themselves around.

Foster Kalama

I remember a case where a kid was told three times to please not do something. My wife works in the school, and she overheard this. The teacher said to the kid, "Why do I have to tell you again?" And the kid turned around and said, "Because I'm brown and you're white." When I talk to Native American kids, I tell them it's time to step up in life from that.

What I mean is, last year we had two hundred and fifty kids missing middle school each day, and half of them were Native Americans. There's three hundred Native American students, so that's a huge number absent each day. I tell them we should be ashamed of that. We can't be just bad statistics. I tell them I am sick of us pointing our fingers at everybody else.

I wrote up a packet explaining our Native American culture of the Wasco, Warm Springs, and Paiute, how we all adopted the same longhouse ways and sweat lodge and all that. I put our hunting and fishing in it, the root digging, everything. The giveaways and feasts and powwows. I explained why some of our kids are tired when they come to school. If there is a funeral, they go to the longhouse, and some of our funerals last a very long time. I made these packets to hand out to teachers, but some of the teachers didn't even want to read it. I'd say a huge majority of our teachers really care about our kids, but a handful don't.

I'd say it's the same with the students. We have over seven hundred students at both schools, and out of the whole bunch, from the fifth all the way to the twelfth grade, there's probably about forty to fifty that get in trouble over and over.

Last year in the middle school, we had over four hundred kids that were suspended—that's counting everybody, not just Native Americans—and it's only been eighty-something this year. We have, I think, five Native American people working in the middle school now, and that's made a lot of things change. My wife got hired this year to help. A lot of people think she was hired because of me, but I didn't have anything to do with it.

My youngest daughter is five years old. Then we've got Timion, who's seven and who's received several awards, including student of the month, and he's had perfect attendance. My nine-year-old son is in the Talented and Gifted program. He's got all kinds of

Traditional Columbia River fisherman BY FOSTER KALAMA

awards, and that makes us feel really great. Those are my three younger ones.

I have an older daughter who's eighteen; she's graduated, and it really hurts me that she's turned toward alcohol. I guess it's probably because she chose a guy who has alcohol and drug problems. I'm just praying that someday she'll pick herself up and start being what she needs to be. I have another son named John Kalama who has his eyes set on the navy.

I never really got to be there at the young ages for my older children because of my alcoholism. I had them at first and then gave them up for four years to my mother. I know they suffered. My oldest daughter was sexually abused, and I think that's why she drank, because that's why I drank. She played on the varsity basketball team just last year, and they went to state. They didn't win state or anything, but they got there.

This year my boy John played on the JV team and did real well the last few games. He's good in school, and our other daughter, Marie, is also a real good student. She swings between the varsity and JV teams, and they're also going to go to state this year. They'll be playing next Tuesday. I guess all the hard work I did with them on the basketball court is showing now. I always watch my kids play. Even after I get done coaching over at the middle school, I go and watch. With my coaching, though, I'll probably have to miss out on the games at state.

I'm also an artist. I do a lot of drawing of our traditional fishermen. I do a lot of pencil drawings and also a lot of carving of elk and deer antlers. My art goes all over. I've got elk antlers to Oklahoma and all the way down to Hawaii. I work on Native American regalia, bustles and headdresses.

I used to do traditional dance. I was a fancy dancer a long time ago, and I used to sing and drum. I traveled from powwow to powwow with a group. We called it Powwow Trail, and we were everywhere. We'd come back long enough to go through the sweat lodge and have our own little ceremonies, and then we'd head out again, from powwow to powwow. We traveled all over the States and up to Canada.

These have been my hobbies. I've hunted elk, deer, and bear. That's my reservation life. I fought with a rattlesnake one time up in the Mutton Mountain area. Fortunately, I won.

Afterword

He didn't know if he was stupid or just like most Indian men he knew. Deep down, he thought, they all wanted their women to take care of them. From what he'd seen, all the reservations across America were the same. The true victims of the reservation system were the men.

Rudy knew the history. When the Army first herded redskins onto reservations, the men could no longer go great distances to hunt, they could not take up the warpath or even practice their old religious ceremonies. Their usefulness died in front of them. They became idle, accepting relief and depending on rations. They discovered alcohol. The women continued to do all the housekeeping chores and child-rearing, but the women also became the true heads of households. They began to wear the pants in the family, even though they still deferred to their men in public. Rudy knew the history.

ADRIAN LOUIS, *Skins*

Anyone who cares about North American Indians knows a fair amount of the history; and because much of that history is bleak, so is most of the honest writing that recounts and analyzes it. A well-known representative example is Dee Brown's *Bury My Heart at Wounded Knee: An Indian History of the American West*, which is a cataloguing of shocking examples of human cruelty.

The past few decades have seen the emergence of a number of notable American Indian poets and writers of both fiction and non-fiction: Vine Deloria Jr., N. Scott Momaday, Hyemeyohsts Storm, James Welch, Adrian Louis, Louis Owens, Sherman Alexie, Leslie Silko, Louise Erdrich, Linda Hogan, and many more. Their works, too, when they are centered on reservation life, tend to dwell for understandable reasons on the negative aspects of that life. "Look at what you've done to us" is the legitimate theme.

Outsiders who write of modern reservation life show the same inclination to dwell on the negative. ("Look at what we've done to them" is their apparent message.) An article by Debra Weyermann in *Harper's Magazine* (April 1998, Vol. 296, No. 1775: 60) is a typical example. Weyermann's specific subject is the murder rate among young people on the twenty-seven-thousand-square-mile Navajo reservation in Arizona, New Mexico, and Utah.

When she visits Navajo Police Captain Randy John for an interview, this is her description: "To get to John's office, I'd driven by a burnt-out grocery store and a crumbling puke-green public housing project that looked like it would blow over in the next good desert windstorm. . . . The floors in John's office were slightly warped, and the metal furniture looked like it came his way fourth-hand from some government agency that had improved its lot in life." Virtually every sentence in the article—every descriptive detail, every narrated incident—is at least as grim in content and tone as this brief example. Though Weyermann's sorrow and concern over modern Navajo life are undoubtedly sincere, her viewpoint merely contributes another predictably depressing chapter to the public portrayal of twentieth-century North American Indians.

Our intent in this book has been to present a more balanced view, and our motive should be obvious: now at the end of the twentieth century, good and hopeful things are happening on Indian reservations, and more Americans need to know about them. The men and women whose interviews are included here—and many more like them in many places—are working hard to preserve their languages and their traditions, and they have clearly achieved some notable successes. Mothers and fathers, grandmothers and grandfathers, teachers and volunteers win thousands of victories, small and large, each day.

But we must also stress that our intent is not to overstate these successes. All too often, unfortunately, this year's victory is obliterated by next year's loss. Alcoholism remains a curse; Indian children continue to be influenced by the worst that the dominant culture has to offer; and if racism among whites is dying, it is not dying nearly so quickly as the salmon runs in coastal rivers.

So, the sad history summarized by Adrian Louis and documented by Dee Brown is undeniably important, as is the tragic violence among today's Navajo youths that Debra Weyermann recounts. But so is the underreported and therefore barely noticed fact (published in March 1999 in the Morbidity and Mortality Weekly Report of the Centers for Disease Control and Prevention) that the number of infant deaths among Northwest Indians has dropped so dramatically in recent years that the rate is now the same as for the rest of the population. Between 1985 and 1988, twenty out of every thousand Indian children in the area died before their first birthdays; between 1993 and 1996, fewer than eight per thousand died. Nearly half of this decline is due to a reduction in Sudden Infant Death Syndrome, brought about because Indian parents have been encouraged not to allow their infants to sleep on their stomachs. Ellie Roush, a pediatric nurse for the Puyallup tribe, adds a telling comment to this particular occurrence: "They were on the right track back in the traditional days, putting [their babies] on baby boards."

The courageous Warm Springs men and women we have talked to—and thousands like them whom we will never know in places we will never visit—are clearly aware of the enduring value of their old traditions: stories, salmon, dances, language, and very much more. They understand that, for them and for their people, a complete future must always include an eternal past.

 From Luther Standing Bear (Lakota):

> *The man from Europe is still a foreigner and an alien. And he still hates the man who questioned his path across the continent.*
>
> *But in the Indian the spirit of the land is still vested; it will be until other men are able to divine and meet its rhythm. Men must be born and reborn to belong.*

From Jim Harrison, *Just Before Dark:*

On the way back from Montana last summer, I stopped at Fort Robinson, Nebraska. The site of the murder of Crazy Horse was closed due to "budget restrictions." I felt a surge of anger akin to a lump of hot coal under the breastbone. The scene of one of the most momentous events in the soul history of the nation was closed while gaggles of tourists wheezed through the cavalry-horse barns. I would gladly have given up my own life to see a few thousand Sioux come over the hill and torch the whole place. You can get consciousness and a conscience free by reading history. It awakens a desire in you, thought by many childish, to see parity on earth with no hope of heaven.

Suggested Reading

HISTORICAL OVERVIEW OF AMERICAN INDIAN AFFAIRS

The purpose of our discussion of American Indian affairs is simply to provide a skeletal context for the specific story of the Warm Springs Reservation and the multiple voices in the interviews. With this in mind, we decided to look just at primary materials to present our perspective on the issues and events leading to the formation of reservations. *The American Indian and the United States: A Documentary History* (Wilcomb E. Washburn, ed.; New York: Random House, 1973) proved to be a far more accessible source of information than the original government documents. Washburn's four-volume documentary includes reports of the Commissioners of Indian Affairs from 1826 to 1963; congressional debates on Indian affairs; acts, ordinances, and proclamations; and Indian treaties and legal decisions.

The State of Native America: Genocide, Colonization, and Resistance (M. Annette Jaimes, ed.; Boston: South End Press, 1992) offers a detailed analysis of the historical relationship between the United States government and the indigenous people of the continent from the perspective of native peoples themselves. Each of the twenty essays in the book is well written and heavily documented. In addition to a table of key Indian laws and cases, the essays cover both general and specific topics, such as the relevance of international laws and politics for the self-determination of indigenous peoples and American Indian fishing rights. Jorge Noriega's essay "American Indian Education" is referenced below in the bibliographic section on education.

HISTORICAL AND CURRENT INFORMATION
ABOUT THE CONFEDERATED TRIBES OF WARM SPRINGS

The People of Warm Springs, produced and published by the Confederated Tribes of the Warm Springs Reservation of Oregon (Warm Springs, 1984), provides the most succinct and accurate history of the Confederated Tribes. This cloth-bound volume contains a number of historical photographs gleaned from the Oregon Historical Society and from members of the Confederated Tribes, as well as color photographs of contemporary reservation scenes and residents. Reading *The People of Warm Springs* is the next best thing to visiting the Warm Springs Museum on the reservation. A number of the tribal historical artifacts pictured in the text, such as the woven cornhusk and hemp root bag and the beaded moccasins, are housed in the museum. Many of the texts for museum displays and dioramas come directly from *The People of Warm Springs* manuscript. What the museum offers that the book cannot reproduce are the video renditions of tribal storytellers recounting myths and stories in Paiute, Wasco, and Sahaptin. Traditional dance ceremonies and scenes of dip-net fishing at Celilo Falls round out the video experience at the museum.

Cynthia D. Stowell's *Faces of a Reservation: A Portrait of the Warm Springs Indian Reservation* (Portland: Oregon Historical Society Press, 1987) not only provides an excellent photographic look at the reservation and the people, but offers insightful commentary on the daily lives of the residents of Warm Springs. Stowell's seven-year residency on the reservation, along with her experiences as a reporter for *Spilyay Tymoo* (Coyote News), give credence to her interpretation of reservation life. The bibliography for *Faces of a Reservation* supports the historical analysis of the cultural and anthropological differences between the Paiute, Wasco, and Warm Springs (Sahaptin) people who make up the Confederated Tribes of the Warm Springs Reservation.

Another excellent source for understanding the distinct cultural backgrounds of the various tribes that comprise the Confederation at Warm Springs is *The First Oregonians* (Carolyn M. Baun and Richard Lewis, eds. Portland: Oregon Council for the Humanities, 1991). In addition to discussions of traditional life ways of Oregon Indians from the coast, the plateau, the western interior, and the basin, *The First Oregonians* also includes a specific chapter, "Giving the Past a Voice: The Confederated Tribes of the Warm Springs Reservation," which highlights the efforts of the reservation's Cultural and Heritage Department to revive native languages and culture at Warm Springs.

Keeping native cultures alive and sharing the rich oral literature of Oregon is Jarold Ramsey's purpose for compiling and editing *Coyote Was Going There: Indian Literature of the Oregon Country* (Seattle: University of Washington Press, 1977). Ramsey has organized the tales by region; the section most pertinent to our study is "Part Two: The Columbia." All twenty-five entries in this section originate from either the Wishram or the Wasco people of the Columbia River, tribes that were relocated in Warm Springs with the 1855 Treaty With Tribes of Middle Oregon, which established the Warm Springs Reservation. Two of these stories, "The Sun Box" and "The Deserted Boy," were particularly important to us in terms of providing a context for the ideas we explore in the historical and education chapters.

AMERICAN INDIAN EDUCATION

Good background reading for a sense of what life at an Indian boarding school was like in mid-nineteenth-century America is Michael Coleman's *American Indian Children at School, 1850–1930* (Jackson: University Press of Mississippi, 1993). Coleman uses autobiographical accounts narrated by adults about their experiences as children in the boarding schools to support his discussion. Coleman has mined the autobiographies for data relating to events that took place decades earlier and measured those accounts against reports written by missionaries and contemporary white sources to substantiate the accuracy of the American Indian view of the boarding school era.

Coleman's portrait of the boarding school experience clearly supports the scathing analysis of American Indian education offered by Jorge Noriega in Chapter XIII of Jaimes's *The State of Native America* (referenced above in the "Historical Overview of American Indian Affairs"). Noriega begins his diatribe against indoctrination for subordination to colonialism with a discussion of the "formal education" of indigenous people of North America by French Jesuit missionaries in 1611. Noriega details the conditions of manual labor schools in the late nineteenth century; he also discusses Indians in the public schools and higher education in modern America.

While Noreiga supplies multiple examples, facts, events, legal decisions, documents, and testimonials to support his concerns, Vine Deloria Jr. builds a strong philosophical case for Indians controlling their own education in *Indian Education in America* (Boulder: American Indian Science and Engineering Society, 1991 and 1994).

Other researched studies and analyses corroborate Deloria's conclusions. Delores J. Huff's *To Live Heroically: Institutional Racism and American Indian Education* (New York: State University of New York Press, 1997) is the most current and best-documented work in this category. Huff is of Cherokee descent and is Professor of American Indian Studies at California State University, Fresno; she formerly served as director of education for the Boston Indian Center and as principal of the Pierre Indian Learning Center in South Dakota. Huff covers such topics as the history and economic impact of institutional racism in this country and the evaluation of schools and teachers. She looks at the impact of racism on local politics, economics, and education.

Margaret Szasz's seminal work, *Education and the American Indian: The Road to Self Determination, 1928–1973* (Albuquerque: University of New Mexico Press, 1974), begins with the Meriam Report in 1928 and continues through the 1969 Kennedy Report and its aftermath. Szasz concentrates on education directed by the Indian Bureau, but also discusses schools controlled by Indian people themselves. She includes a brief history of the role of the federal government in public schooling for Indian children.

Building on Szasz's work, Guy B. Senese, in *Self-Determination and the Social Education of Native Americans* (New York: Praeger Publishers, 1991), critiques the manipulation of the Self-Determination and Education Assistance Act to create the illusion of Indian control of Indian schools.

OTHER WORKS THAT CONTAINED INSIGHTFUL PASSAGES

Baughman, Michael. *Mohawk Blood.* New York: Lyons and Burford, 1995.

Brown, Dee. *Bury My Heart at Wounded Knee.* New York: Holt, Rinehart and Winston, 1971.

Coles, Robert. *Eskimos, Chicanos, Indians.* Boston: Little, Brown, 1977.

Harden, Blaine. *A River Lost.* New York: W. W. Norton, 1996.

Harrison, Jim. *Just Before Dark.* Boston: Houghton Mifflin, 1992.

Lesley, Craig. *River Song.* Boston: Houghton Mifflin, 1989.

Louis, Adrian C. *Skins.* New York: Crown Publishers, 1995.

Matthiessen, Peter. *At Play in the Fields of the Lord.* New York: Random House, 1965.

————. *In the Spirit of Crazy Horse.* New York: Viking Penguin, 1992.

Momaday, N. Scott. "The Man Made of Words." In *Indian Voices: The First Convocation of American Indian Scholars.* San Francisco: The Indian History Press, 1970.

Index

Act of February 15, 1929, 141
Alexie, Sherman, 161
American Indian education (general),
    133–139, 141–144. *See also* Warm
    Springs Reservation: education
American Indian Movement (AIM), 7
Army Corps of Engineers, 22

Belloni, Robert (judge), 27
Boldt, George (judge), 27
Bonneville Dam, 44
Brant, Joseph (Mohawk chief), 2
Brown, Dee, 161, 163
Bureau of Indian Affairs, 18, 19, 141, 142
Bury My Heart at Wounded Knee, 161
Buslach, Wanda, 145

Campbell, John M., 32
Carlisle Indian School, 136
Castro, Rupert, 5–7
Celilo Falls, 14, 15, 22–24, 27, 29, 30, 33,
    44
    "Last Days at Celilo" (video), 29
Chemawa Indian School, 140
Cherokee Nation, 17
Choctaw Academy, 136
Chinookan language, 14
"Clean Streams" Initiative, 26
Clinton administration, 26
Clinton, Bill, 27
Cole, William, 29
Collier, John, 142
Columbia River
    dams, 4, 22, 25, 26, 27, 34
    native fishing on, 4, 13, 14, 54, 56,
      150
    salmon and steelhead runs, 4, 11,
      21, 22, 24, 25, 31, 35, 116

Columbia River Inter-Tribal Fish
    Commission, 26, 27, 55
Committee of One Hundred, 141
Crazy Horse, 7, 164
Culture and Heritage Committee, 145
Custer, South Dakota, 7

Dalles Dam, 22, 23, 24, 30, 44
Dances with Wolves, 10
Delacruz, Joe (Quinalt leader), 5
Deloria, Vine, Jr., 134, 135, 161
Deschutes River
    fishing, 1, 2, 8, 35
    and irrigation and livestock, 4
    photo of, 3

Education and the American Indian, 134
Endangered Species Act, 28
Erdrich, Louise, 161

Florendo, Brent, 10, 11
    storytelling of, 22
Fund for the Republic Commission
    on the Rights, Liberties and Re-
    sponsibilities of the American
    Indians, 143

General Allotment Act (Dawes Act),
    19
Graham, Arlene, 122
Grand Coulee Dam, 27
Grand Ronde River, 26
Grant, Ulysses, 15
Gray's Sporting Journal, 33

Hardin, Blaine, 25
Harper's Magazine, 162
Head Start, 142

Hells Canyon Dam, 27
Henry, Ashley, 25
Herring, Elbert, 18
Hogan, Linda, 161
Howard, General O. O., 15
Huff, Dolores, 141, 143
Hungry Summer, The, 32

Indian Reorganization Act of 1934
    (Wheeler-Howard Act), 16, 19, 142
Indian Self-Determination and
    Education Assistance Act, 142
Inouye, Daniel, 56
Ishi (Yahi Indian), 5

John, Peter, 33, 34
John Day River, 24, 26
Johnson O'Malley Act, 142

Kah-Nee-Ta Lodge, 8, 29, 99, 130, 145
    photo of, 9
Kennedy, Robert, 143
Kitzhaber, John, 26, 27

Latimer, Douglas, 5–7
Louis, Adrian, 10, 161, 163

Madras, 37, 49, 70, 84, 115, 123, 124, 128,
    140, 143, 147, 151
    photo of, 49
Matthiessen, Peter, 10
Meriam Report, 141
Minnick, Ralph, 145
Momaday, N. Scott, 5, 161

National Congress of American
    Indians, 143
National Marine Fisheries Service,
    28
Natural Resources Department
    (tribal), 56
Navajo Reservation, 162
Nez Percé Indians, 27
Niatum, Duane, 5
Noriega, Jorge, 135
Northwest Ordinance (1787), 17

Office of Economic Opportunity, 143
Office of Indian Affairs, 17

Owens, Louis, 161
Owens, Robert, 5

Pacific Northwest Utilities Confer-
    ence Committee, 25
Paiute Indians, 4, 15, 16, 31
    language of, 74, 146
    peace treaty (1868), 15
Pine Creek Ranch, 26
Pine Ridge Reservation, 7
Pistolhead, Elsie, 14
Portland *Oregonian*, 26, 28, 74, 75

Rainbow Market, 2, 48, 50
    photo of, 3
Ramsey, Jarold, 12
Red Wind Foundation, 108
Removal Act, 18
Ryan, W. Carson, 141

Sahaptin language, 14, 24, 74, 146
Santos, Susana, 29
Sapir, Edward, 139
Senate Select Subcommittee on
    Indian Education, 143
Senese, Guy, 144
Seven Arrows, 5, 6
Shawaway, Myra, 122, 146
Sherars Falls, 54
Shoshonean language, 15
Silko, Leslie, 161
Simnasho, 122, 123, 129
Snake River, 27
Spilyay Tymoo (Coyote News), 8, 144,
    145, 146
State of Native America, The, 135
Storm, Hyemeyohsts, 5, 6, 161
Strong, Ted, 27, 28
Szasz, Margaret, 134

Tenino people, 24
Thorpe, Jim, 136
To Live Heroically, 141
Treaty of 1855, 13, 14, 27, 139

Udall Task Force, 143
Umatilla Indians, 27
U.S. Department of Justice, 18
U.S. Fish and Wildlife Service, 56

Index

Warm Springs Elementary School,
    114, 118–131, 140, 145
    photo of, 120
Warm Springs Indians, 1, 2, 4, 11, 13–16,
    18, 19, 24, 26, 31, 33
    myths of, 12, 137–139
    storytelling of, 13
Warm Springs Museum, 29, 72, 73
    photo of, 55
Warm Springs Reservation, 3, 8, 15, 16,
    19, 31, 39–41, 44, 45
    alcoholism, 58–63
    Children's Protective Services, 125
    crime and law enforcement,
        92–105
    education, 77, 78, 80–91, 139, 140,
        144–147

health issues, 64–70
Pi-Ume-Sha Treaty Days, 70
Tribal Council, 25, 48, 49, 86, 92,
    93, 97, 98, 126, 152
Tribal Court, 16
Warm Springs River, 8, 150
War on Poverty, 144
Wasco Indians, 4, 13–16, 24, 30, 31, 74
    language of, 74, 146
Welch, James, 5, 161
Weyermann, Debra, 162, 163
Wishram Texts, 139
Work, Hubert, 141
Wounded Knee, 7
Wright, Al, 25

Yakama Indians, 26, 27